100 WAYS TO WIN A TENNER

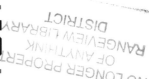

First published in 2003
This edition published by Carlton Books Ltd in 2018

Text, design and illustrations © Carlton Books Limited 2018

A CIP catalogue record for this book is available from the
British Library.

ISBN 978-1-78739-137-6

Managing Editor: Luke Friend
Design & Project Art Direction: Darren Jordan
Illustrations: Peter Liddiard, Sudden Impact Media; Darren Jordan
Photography: P12: Mark Bennett
Production: Emily Noto

10 9 8 7 6 5 4 3 2 1

Printed in China

100 WAYS TO WIN A TENNER

SIMPLE TRICKS TO FOOL YOUR FRIENDS AND BEAT THE ODDS

CARLTON
BOOKS

CONTENTS

THREE SPORTING CHANCE

CAN'T SHUFFLE A PACK WITHOUT PLAYING 52 CARD PICK UP? NEVER PICKED UP A POOL CUE IN YOUR LIFE? FUMBLE NO MORE. HERE ARE THE REAL SECRETS OF THE SHARPS, SHARKS AND HUSTLERS; WITHOUT ANY SKILL WHATSOEVER YOU'LL BE ABLE TO BEAT THE EXPERTS AT THEIR OWN GAME.

FOUR MASTERMIND

DO YOU HIDE EVERY TIME A PUB QUIZ STARTS OR SOMEONE SUGGESTS A GAME OF TRIVIAL PURSUIT? NOT ANY MORE. CONCEAL YOUR IGNORANCE WITH THESE TRICKY QUESTIONS GUARANTEED TO PUZZLE YOUR OPPONENT, KNOCK THE QUIZMASTER OFF HIS PERCH AND EARN YOU ENOUGH MONEY TO PAY FOR A PROPER EDUCATION.

FIVE PARTY ANIMAL

CAN'T SING, CAN'T DANCE? DON'T WORRY, THESE SCAMS AND SWINDLES ARE DESIGNED TO MAKE YOU THE LIFE AND SOUL OF THE PARTY, WINNING THE ADMIRATION OF THE MASSES AT THE SAME TIME AS THEIR HARD-EARNED DOSH.

CONTENTS 2

THE DRINKS ARE ON YOU

TIPPED OFF

SPORTING CHANCE

MASTERMIND

PARTY ANIMAL

DEDICATION

This book is dedicated to Bill Thompson of the House of Secrets, Blackpool, England, friend and mentor for the past thirty years and the nicest bloke you're ever likely to meet. Thanks Bill.

"SON, NO MATTER HOW FAR YOU TRAVEL AND HOW MUCH YOU SEE,
SOMEDAY, SOMEWHERE, SOME GUY IS GOING TO COME UP TO YOU WITH
A BRAND NEW DECK OF CARDS ON WHICH THE SEAL HAS NEVER EVEN
BEEN BROKEN, AND HE IS GOING TO OFFER TO BET YOU THAT THE QUEEN OF
HEARTS WILL JUMP OUT OF THAT DECK AND SQUIRT CIDER IN YOUR EAR.
BUT SON, DO NOT BET WITH THIS MAN FOR, AS SURE AS YOU DO, YOU ARE
GOING TO END UP WITH AN EAR FULL OF CIDER." - DAMON RUNYAN

INTRODUCTION

Paul Zenon's *100 Ways to Win a Tenner* is a comprehensive guide to scams and swindles that will make you a winner every time. Unlike magic tricks, these bets and stunts use everyday objects and require no skill – just a lot of front. Within minutes you too can be the life and scourge of the party, scamming the pants off everyone in sight!

They say that cheats never prosper. Unfortunately (or rather fortunately, now that you're in possession of this book), that just ain't true. Most likely it was a rumour put about to ease the mind of some poor sucker who had just lost for the umpteenth time in a rigged game of cards. The real truth is that, armed with the right knowledge, a cheat will always win. He doesn't take chances. What he does take is your money, quicker than you can say I.O.U.

Paul Zenon is the UK's favourite fun loving criminal. Over the years he has worked variously as magician, comedian, croupier and small-time conman. He has spent a lifetime hanging out with and studying the techniques of a rogue's gallery of tricksters, fraudsters, sharks, shysters, and snake-oil sellers. In this, his insider's guide, he spills the beans, tips the tricks of his trade and gives us a crash course in cheating – cheating at cards, at pool and in pub quizzes, drinking games and bar bets, in fact anywhere and everywhere that you can corner a punter into chancing their hard-earned dosh on what seems like a perfectly fair bet. Of course there's no such thing as a fair bet – at least not in this book. Every game and wager is rigged in your favour. And why not? Casinos and bookies have been doing it for years. Remember that knowledge is power, and this is knowledge that is hard come by. Use it wisely! ♠

ONE
THE DRINKS ARE ON YOU

"NEVER GIVE A SUCKER
AN EVEN BREAK."
- PHINEAS T. BARNUM

 BOTTOMS UP

THE HOOK

Few people know it but you are the world's fastest drinker. No, really. Your friends aren't convinced but you keep on bragging until they're sick of hearing about it.

"Okay then, a fiver says I'm a sight faster than you. In fact, a fiver says I can drink three pints before you can even drink three shots!"

Few people can resist a bet, especially when they've had a few sherbets. So it won't be long before someone takes you up on your challenge.

"And just to make it interesting," you say "the loser pays for all the drinks as well – fair enough?"

So, how exactly are you going to drink three pints before your friend drinks the same number of shots? Very easily is the answer.

THE CATCH

Get the drinks lined up in two rows and then crank up the pressure.

"Are you sure you can afford it?" No-one likes to feel cheap and no-one likes to back down after accepting a challenge.

"Well, let's make it a tenner then." You've cornered him now, but there will be a trickle of suspicion running through his mind so you reassure him, while at the same time setting up the very rules that will make you a winner.

"And just to make sure everything's fair, we're not allowed to touch each other's glasses, or one-another; no nudging elbows or anything like that. And no-one else is allowed to touch either of us or our glasses. To give me a sporting chance, the only thing I'd ask is that you let me finish my first pint before you start on the shots. Is that okay?"

Of course it's okay. You couldn't possibly manage another two pints in the time he can down three teeny shots, especially when you've just necked one.

Next step: *get the money*. This is an essential part of any scam. Hand over your cash to a neutral party and get your opponent to do the same. It's another rule of the bar bet. No one likes to pay, so see the colour of the money first.

Now you're ready. Get Mr. Neutral to shout "Go!" and as soon as you hear it pick up your first pint and down it as fast as you can. Down in one – don't drown yourself. As soon as you have finished, put your glass upside down right over one of his full shot glasses. Now you can take your time drinking the remaining two pints. You've already won.

Why? Because you made the rule that no one could touch any of the glasses. Since your glass is covering one of his – which you didn't touch – he can never down that final shot.

Enjoy the rest of the night.

2 QUIDS IN

THE HOOK

There's no football on the telly, the karaoke machine is bust and it's Sam the barmaid's day off. The pub couldn't get any duller. At least that's what you thought until Sid 'The Kid' walks in and starts telling everyone about how many dodgy motors he's sold that day. If he'd turned the clocks back any further that Cavalier would have had to have been driven by cavaliers. But all is not lost; he's got a few quid on him and you, due to a horse with three legs being unexpectedly entered into the 3.30 at Kempton Park, are brassic. Time to replenish your funds.

You take your last tenner out of your pocket, roll it up, throw it high in the air and catch it in your empty pint glass. And you keep doing it until you've caught Sid's attention. And when he asks what the hell you're playing at, you say "Just practising."

"Practising for what, being sectioned?"

"Practising catching this tenner in this glass. Bloke in the Fool and Bladder said it couldn't be done."

"Said what couldn't be done?" asks Sid.

"Said I couldn't throw the tenner three feet in the air and catch it in this glass. Said he'd give me a tenner for everyone I could do."

"Looks easy to me," says Sid, understandably puzzled.

"Nah, takes coordination. I bet you couldn't do it."

Sid looks at you as if you are stupid. And as soon as you get that look you follow through, saying "In fact, I'll give you a quid for every note you catch."

It sounds foolhardy but it's a bet you can't lose.

THE CATCH

Get Sid to open his wallet, take out some tenners and screw them up into balls. Arrange them along the bar. Now borrow some pint glasses from the barmaid and put one next to each rolled up note. Meanwhile, you will also need to get some pound coins. Yes, you will be paying out, but no you won't be losing.

The bet is exactly as you said it would be. Sid has to throw each note at least three feet in the air and then catch it in a pint glass.

At the end of the session, he'll probably have all the notes in all the glasses. Take each glass in turn and pour out the notes. Count them aloud and then announce the score.

"That's six you got in the glasses. Brilliant. And like I said, I'll give you a quid for every one you caught. Here's your six quid mate."

Push six pound coins towards him and then add "And I guess these are mine. Like I said, a quid for every one."

The laughter of everyone's ridicule should drown out his protests. This place seems to be getting a bit livelier at last. But time to move on. There are a dozen bars to visit and a sucker like Sid in every one of them.

3 UNDER COVER OPERATION

THE HOOK

You don't have to play every bet for big money. Sometimes it's easier to take it off 'em in copper and silver rather than wads of crinklies. This one will keep you in free drinks all night if only because your mates will watch it over and over again as new people join your group.

While you are waiting for the rest of your motley crew to arrive at the bar, make the following wager with whoever seems to be the most gullible. Jim's always a good bet. His parents didn't give him an easy-to-spell name for nothing. "Did you know Jim that these tables are really porous?" Knock on the table as if testing the wood.

"Porous?" says Jim, genuinely interested because it's a rare day when anyone addresses him by name.

"Porous. Liquid goes right through it like a sponge. I'll show you what I mean."

You take Jim's whisky and Coke — he's a slow drinker and one short usually lasts him all night — and you place it in the centre of the table. Then you say "Wait there a minute", go to the bar and borrow a cocktail shaker, ice bucket, vase, anything that is non see-through and which will fit over the glass.

Jim will wonder what you are doing placing an ice bucket over his drink, but he won't have to wonder for too long; here's the pitch: "I bet you a quid that I can drink that whisky and Coke without lifting the bucket — won't touch the bucket, won't move the bucket, won't do anything at all to it. But I'll drink your drink."

Even Jim, the most cautious guy this side of a minefield, will have to concede that this is impossible and might just be worth a quid of his money to see. With a nudge and a hint that "it's only for fun", you'll soon have him begging you to prove your claim. And, amazingly, you can.

THE CATCH

When Jim produces his money and places it alongside yours on the table, you reiterate your boast: "I won't touch the bucket. Won't lift the bucket. Won't move the bucket. Neither will anyone else. That clear?" Crystal. You then dive under the table and proceed to make the most disgusting slurping noises you can. Jim will start to think about the "porous" wood remark you made earlier. Surely you can't be drinking it through the wood. Can you?

Come back up smacking your lips and saying "next time don't drown it with so much Coke." Sit down, like the smug man that you are, pick up the money from the table and gaze off into the distance. It might take a minute or two but curiosity is an impatient bedfellow and Jim will have no option but to lift the bucket to see if his drink is still there.

It is. But Jim has unwittingly done you the favour of removing the bucket. Quickly, pick up the glass and down its contents in one. You've made good on your promise and drunk the whisky without touching the bucket. Let's hope he didn't really drown it with Coke.

That's a quid and a drink to you. What's more, Jim will be more than happy for you to play the same trick for the rest of the night on every person that comes anywhere near; it'll help him to feel less of a sucker himself. Until next time that is.

4 DOWN AND OUT

THE HOOK

Poor Jim. He was the first to be taken and now he's going to be the last. There should be a law against it really, but fortunately there isn't.

He's been watching you closely, betting everyone that you can drink their drinks without touching that there bucket. If only he had the front to do that, he's thinking. In fact that's what everyone who's lost money to you will be thinking. Perhaps they'll try it themselves one day.

Well, no time like the present. The bar's about to close and 'time' has been called. You lean over to Jim and say, "You've got to give it a try Jim. You'll regret it if you don't."

"You reckon?"

"You've watched me do it all night haven't you?"

"Yes but...."

"No buts Jim. This night is yours."

And with that you pull over a total stranger who is carrying his drink from the bar. "Hey, excuse me, but you've just got to see this. My mate here's got a fantastic trick, haven't you Jim?"

THE CATCH

As I said, poor Jim. Nervously he repeats your proposition to a man he's never met before. And he claims that he can drink the man's drink even though it is hidden under that bucket. He won't lift the bucket, won't move the bucket, won't touch the bucket. And here's the pound to say he can do it.

Be gentle. It's Jim's first time. Help him set the bucket over the stranger's drink and give him a nod of reassurance just before he ducks under the table and starts to make his slurping noises.

But as soon as he does, you raise your finger to your lips and shush the crowd as you quietly lift the bucket. Now, you quickly down the drink and replace the bucket.

Jim resurfaces to a smiling crowd. He thinks he's pulled off the trick successfully. Until the stranger, your instant stooge, lifts the bucket. No-one is more stunned than Jim to find the glass empty. I've seen punters speechless when they discover that the drink has indeed disappeared from beneath that bucket. Which is just as well, considering the world of pain they are about to enter as they try to explain the trick away.

5 SIX SHOOTER

THE HOOK

What I like about bar bets is that they are all about lateral thinking. And, fortunately for us, after a couple of beers most people can't even spell the phrase, never mind put it into action.

Most bar bets are simple puzzles. Stuff a kid could solve. But the best ones are not so much brain teasers as devices to encourage public humiliation of an individual whilst simultaneously emptying their wallet. Take this one for instance.

You take six shot glasses, three of them full and three of them empty. And you arrange them in a line so that the three full glasses are on the left of the row and the three empty glasses on the right. So far so easy. But here's the wager.

"I bet you a tenner, you can't move the glasses around so that they alternate, full/empty/full/empty all the way along the row." To demonstrate what you mean, you openly rearrange the glasses so that they do indeed alternate full/empty. Seems easy. You did it, why can't they?

The reason is simple. You just shuffled the glasses around but to win the bet they are only allowed to move one of them. Alternate the glasses by only moving one glass. Looks impossible but it's not. Still, it'll cost them a tenner to find out how to do it. Loser pays for the drinks, too. No prizes for guessing who that's going to be.

THE CATCH

I regret to say that this is simplicity itself. It's that lateral thinking I mentioned earlier. To win, all you need do is lift up the centre one of the full glasses and pour its contents into the centre glass of the empty ones. Hey presto, the glasses now alternate.

6 THREES UP

THE HOOK

The six glasses in *Six Shooter* might prove too much for some folks. Six is a big number if you've had a skinful of Old Scrotum's Special or whatever the real ale anoraks have christened beer of the week. So try this, with just three shot glasses.

Take the three glasses and arrange them in a line on the table. When someone asks what you are doing say "It's a sobriety test. Copper once showed it to me." Quickly you take two of the glasses, one in each

hand, and flip them over top to bottom. Then you do it again, switching glasses. And then a third time. All the glasses finish mouth uppermost. "See? Sober as a judge."

The lawman in question must have been Judge Pickled because as your mates know, you've had more than your fair share for the evening. Still, you set the glasses up again and start turning them two at a time until they're once again all mouth uppermost. "Ready to be filled" you point out.

"Fancy another?"

They certainly do, and that's when you decide to make things a little more interesting. "Tell you what. If you pass the sobriety test, I'll get the drinks. Better still, I'll give you a tenner and you can go and get them yourself. But if you don't pass it, the drinks are on you."

The so-called test seems to consist of nothing more than turning glasses over two at a time, three times in total, so that they all end up mouth uppermost.

They've seen you do it twice – it looks dead easy – and they will already be feeling confident. But to make sure, you do it a third time, saying, "It's really very simple. You just have to turn two glasses at a time and you're only allowed three turns. All glasses ready to be filled at the finish. Got that? Okay, who wants to give it a go?"

Well who could possibly refuse a simple challenge like that? No one whose already filled up on Old Scrotum's Special that's for sure.

THE CATCH

This is a real classic of the genre and many a sober man has found his wallet lightened because of it. That's because you cheat.

You begin by demonstrating how simple the test is with the three glasses in a row as shown. The middle one is mouth upwards and the outer ones are mouth downwards.

 Make your first move by taking glasses B and C, one in each hand, and turning them over at the same time.

 Make your second move by turning over glasses A and C.

 Make your third and final move by turning over glasses B and C. That brings all three glasses mouth up.

You can repeat these moves several times but do it quickly as if you are trying to confuse them. Once they think they have it, you put the glasses back in their starting position. At least you appear to.

In fact you put them in the totally opposite position to the one you started with. The middle one mouth downwards and the end two mouth up.

If your victim starts with the glasses in this arrangement, there is no way he can bring the glasses mouth up in three moves. Which, as always, means he'll be the one filling the glasses. Enjoy.

HIGH SPIRITS

THE HOOK

Some things are worth paying to see. Really! This is one bet that everyone will be trying the day after you show it to them. It just seems so amazing that it works at all. Makes you wish you'd paid more attention in science class.

"Here's something you'll never forget," you say, taking a shot glass full of whisky and a shot glass full of water and placing them on the bar. "Do you think that I can get the whisky and the water to change places, just like that?!"

Let your victim consider it for a moment. He'll have a dozen questions and you can answer them all honestly.

"No, what I'm saying is that I can make the whisky and the water change places. And I'm not going to do it by pouring the whisky into another glass. In fact I won't use any other glasses. Just these two here."

Pause while the victim considers the options and then eventually tells you that frankly he can't see you making good on that claim. That's the time to hit him with a friendly wager. Friendly as in 'friendly fire'.

"Well, ten quid says I can. Ten quid says I can get the whisky from this glass into that. And the water from that glass into this." Put your tenner on the table, a direct challenge to his manhood.

Now the first thing anyone wants to do is avoid risking any money. But this is a money game. No money, no miracle. So don't be tempted to give a free show. You're not a registered charity. Instead, turn the whole thing around. Tell him that he was the one who didn't believe you could do it, and if that's the way he feels he should put his money where his mouth is. In other words, wind him up until you hear the spring strain, because when he finally puts his cash on the table, it's as good as yours.

THE CATCH

As I said before, he'll probably thank you for this one. All you need to do it besides the glasses of whisky and water is a slim laminated membership card of some sort. Doesn't matter what it is as long as it is waterproof and big enough to cover the mouth of one of the glasses.

Here's what you do. First of all, make sure that the whisky glass is full to the brim. The glass of water should be filled just shy of the top.

Now place the laminated card over the mouth of the whisky glass. Very carefully lift the glass and card together and turn them upside down. The card keeps the whisky in the glass. Place the whisky glass and card over the glass of water.

Make sure the glasses are aligned perfectly. Now slowly and gradually

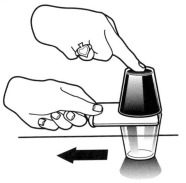

move the card to one side so that a tiny opening appears between the glasses on the inside. The miracle that follows is guaranteed to amaze even cynical old you. You see, the whisky is heavier than the water, and it will begin to seep into the lower glass. In response, the water will be forced into the upper glass. Incredible as it may seem, the whisky and water are changing place before your very eyes. David Copperfield would be proud of you.

When all the whisky is in the bottom glass, pick up your winnings and buy yourself a well-earned drink.

8 UP AND AWAY

THE HOOK

"It can't be done," you say to your friends around the bar. "It just can't." You have, of course, carefully engineered this conversation for the benefit of Mike who happened to be passing at the very moment. You wouldn't have bothered were it not for the fact that you heard Mike had a nice bit of luck on a filly at Chepstow and has so much sweet folding in his pocket that he fairly rustles as he walks.

"It just can't be done," you say again. Mike has stopped and is looking at you as if you can't be trusted, which, of course, you can't. He's wary of your games but a man who has just won on the gee gees tends to think himself invincible when it comes to the laws of probability. And anyway, he'll only pour all his winnings into that fruit machine, so really you're about to do him and the economy a big favour by keeping his money in circulation for a little longer. Leastways, that's how we like to think of it.

"Mike, it's simple. I say that you can't lift a shot of whisky from the table without spilling a drop." It's a stupid claim. Anyone can do that thinks Mike, what's the catch?"

"No catch. I bet you ten pounds that I can place a glass of whisky on the bar, right here, and you can't lift it without spilling a drop. No catch, but there are conditions."

Mike wonders what they are, expecting something tricky as usual.

"No tricks. Conditions are you only use one hand and you lift the drink straight up. Just reach out and lift the drink up, like this."

You demonstrate with the empty glass. Mike thinks about it. And you turn that thought into wager by saying, "I'll even buy the whisky, and you can have it after the bet, win or lose. Can't say fairer than that."

"All you've got to do is lift up the glass of whisky without spilling any. How does that sound?"

With a pocketful of money it doesn't sound too bad, especially as you are buying the whisky. At least he can console himself with that if he loses. Can't he?

THE CATCH

Poor Mike. He doesn't even get to drink the whisky in this one.

Have the glass filled with a single shot of whisky and place it on the bar. Repeat the conditions of the bet, reminding Mike and everyone else that he must only use one hand and lift the glass straight up. Get him to say that he understands and accepts the wager. And make sure he hands over his tenner to a third party for safekeeping because after he has seen what is going to happen he might not appreciate the way you won.

With everything set, you quickly take out the laminated card you used in *High Spirits*, place it on top of the glass, invert it and set the glass on the bar top. Now carefully slide the laminated card from underneath it. There is now an upside-down glass of whisky on the bar. And there's no way that Mike can lift it without spilling its contents everywhere. Told you Mike wouldn't be getting that drink. You, however, are perfectly entitled to his tenner.

A good tip is to have a bar towel handy when you perform this stunt – there's going to be a certain amount of mopping up to do when that glass eventually gets lifted, and you don't want to be making life difficult for the barman; in the world of the pub blagger he's an essential ally.

9 FOLLOW THE LEADER

THE HOOK

The evening is in full swing, it's your round next, and your wallet is distinctly on the anorexic side. You pick on a likely victim and suggest that the two of you play a drinking game – everyone loves a drinking game and it can be a great decoy for a full-on scam. Loser pays for the next round, obviously.

"It's very simple," you explain. "All you've got to do is follow what I do. Ready?" Although no contracts have been signed, your about-to-be-suckered friend is already nodding their head. After all, it would be churlish not to play along.

"Okay, pick up your glass." They do but you make sure they pick it up in exactly the same way you do. "Pay attention. You've got to follow me exactly. Pick the glass up in your right hand. Remember, loser buys the drinks."

Having got them under starters orders you take them through a simple and slightly bizarre ritual. You raise your glass of beer to the heavens and shout "To Odin!" They follow suit.

Then you raise the glass to the right and shout "To the sun!" They do the same.

You raise your glass to the left and shout "To the moon!" And again, like a sheep, they follow.

Then you bring the glass to your lips and take a big swig. So does your drinking buddy.

You raise your glass once again, shouting "To the Mighty Thor!" and for no good reason so does your mate. Then raise the glass to the right saying, "To the rain!" and then to the left "To the wind!"

Then you take another sip. And raise the glass once more directly in front of you – but this time say nothing.

And no matter how closely your friend has been following you, they will not be able to follow the next move. The lemming has been driven to the edge of the cliff and is about to be given a nudge.

THE CATCH

This is beautifully simple. When you take that last mouthful of beer, keep it in your mouth – do not swallow it. That's why when you raise the glass a third time you don't say anything. You can't – your mouth is full. And that's what makes the last move possible.

Raise the drink again to the right and then to the left. Then slowly bring it back, hold it in front of your mouth and spit the beer back out in a stream into the glass. Your victim won't be able to duplicate this, having automatically swallowed theirs. That next round is in the bin.

 TWICE SHY

THE HOOK

The saying that a little knowledge is a dangerous thing is no more true than when it comes to bar bets. There you are having a top time in the local when trouble arrives in the shape of Smartarse Stan. It was all going so well – you've managed to pull three or four of your favourite stunts and never had to open your wallet once. You're drinking for free and enjoying every minute of it. But here comes Stan. The same Stan that watched you go through your entire repertoire of scams and swindles just a week ago. Stan, who lost not once, not twice, but three times to your shenanigans and only paid up when your mate Mad Mike threatened to use him as a bar towel. Yes, Stan is here, clued up and looking for revenge. But there's no man so blind as knows a little. And with that in mind you invite the whole group to play *Follow the Leader*.

Stan, with a glint in his eye, will assume you have forgotten that he was one of the losers in the *Follow The Leader* game not a week ago. He knows its secret and, sure of winning and gaining revenge, he happily plays along.

Glasses are raised and toasts made. First to Odin then the sun and the moon. Then to the Mighty Thor and the wind and the rain. And then you drink and spit and everyone laughs. All except for Stan, because Stan spits too. He grins triumphantly – he's won! Oh no he hasn't.

THE CATCH

The reason Stan won't win is that you then unexpectedly raise the glass again. You raise it high in the air then make another silent toast to the right and then to the left. You bring the glass to your lips once again and then, to Stan's amazement and intense irritation, spurt out a second stream of beer.

The explanation is simple. First time around you only spit out half of your mouthful. But Stan spat out all of his. He's cashed his chips in early, so to speak, leaving you the victor. The moral of the story is never try to con a conman.

 11 BOTTLE BANK

THE HOOK

One sure way of getting money out of a punter is to offer to show him how to do a trick with it. Now he has no excuse. If he wants to see the trick, he has to put up the cash. The cash in this case is our old mate the ubiquitous ten pound note, which you take from him as you explain the rules of the game.

"It's a game of skill," you say, lying. "Some people can do it, some people can't. I can do it but I'll bet you can't."

You are being deliberately arrogant. No one likes a smartarse, especially when they're in possession of their tenner. "In fact, I'm so sure that you can't do it, I'm prepared to bet you a tenner. I'll put up my tenner against yours."

At this stage the punter might like to see the colour of your money. Take out a note and hand it to a completely independent third party; preferably your best mate. No point taking any chances.

Put the punter's tenner flat on the table and then borrow an empty beer bottle, turn it upside-down and stand it mouth downwards on the ten pound note. The bottle should be on the centre of the note, pinning it down on the table.

"Here's the bet. All you have to do is whip the ten pound note free without knocking over the bottle. You can touch the note but you're not allowed to touch the bottle. Now I'm warning you it's difficult so be careful. Bob – better move to one side because from where I'm standing it looks like you're in the direct line of fire."

"To make it fair, I'll give you three chances, okay? The only thing is, remember you can't touch the bottle."

Whether it is okay or not, the punter's note is stuck under the bottle and if he wants it back, he's got to take you up on your bet.

Giving him three chances to snatch the note from under the bottle without knocking it over may seem a bit generous. It's not. If he's depending on pure skill or a knack to get his money back, he's going to fail. Brains are what are needed here but if you've chosen your victim correctly, you'll have picked someone that doesn't have an excess of grey matter.

THE CATCH

It's all a matter of suggestion. When you made the bet you talked about whipping away the note. You asked Bob to stand back in order to avoid any accident involving high-speed flying glassware. And, you might even have jerked your hand back to suggest a possible reckless attempt to yank the note free. Subliminal suggestion, all of it. The punter will never be able to pull the note free.

Slow stealth is what is required. After the punter has toppled the bottle three times, you prove it can be done as follows.

You very carefully start to roll up the note at one of the short ends. Take is slow and easy and continue rolling the note until it meets the bottle. Move slower still as you continue rolling. You'll be surprised to see that the bottle is pushed by the rolled up portion of the tenner, little by little, along the length of the note until it finally slides off the far end, coming to rest on the tabletop. The note is free. It's also yours. Cheers.

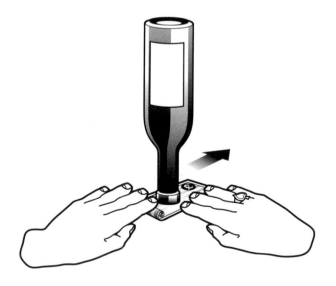

12 MOUTH TO MOUTH

THE HOOK

They say money talks but all it's saying to your victims is "Bye." Here's another slim chance for them to win back what was already theirs to start with.

This time you'll need two empty beer bottles in addition to another borrowed ten pound note. You stand one of the bottles on the table and then place the note on top of it. Makes sure it's a nice clean note, not one that's wrinkled beyond recognition. On top of the note, you place the second bottle, mouth to mouth with the first. The note is trapped between them.

The bet is the same as before. If the punter can get the note free, he can claim one of yours along with it. If he doesn't, you take his. Once again he's not allowed to touch the bottles, only the note.

If the punter has already seen you work *Bottle Bank* he might be tempted to try the rolling-up manoeuvre. If so, good luck to him. I've never got it to work. He might even try to yank the note free, in the

traditional tablecloth-from-under-the-crockery style. If the note was held by the bottles near one of its ends, that might work. But it isn't. The note is trapped at its very centre. If anyone does intend to depend on their cat-like reflexes to whip the note away, you'd be advised to post fielders around the table to catch the flying debris.

THE CATCH

Brains score over brawn once again in this money-grabbing caper. It's perfectly true that any attempt to tug the note from between the two bottles will pretty much be guaranteed to result in failure. But remember what I said about it working if the note was gripped just by its edge? Well, that's the secret of the stunt.

When it comes to your turn you gently and openly tear right across the note. Now the bottles do grip it near its newly ripped edge.

Grip the trapped note at the other end with the thumb and forefinger of one hand. You need a really firm grip.

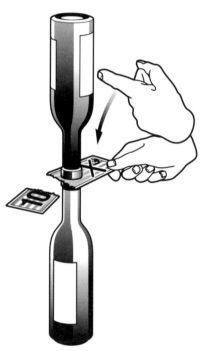

Extend the forefinger of the other hand and bring it down sharply with a chopping motion on the new middle of the note. If you do it fast and clean the note will be snapped away and the bottles will remain standing.

Your reward for this feat of dexterity is in two pieces but a strip of Sellotape will soon put that right. The ten pound note will certainly be easier to mend than your victim's ego.

One last word of warning. This swindle takes practice. So do make sure you try it at home before you attempt it in public. Unless I'm in the bar, of course. I like a good laugh.

⑬ CRASH THE ASH

THE HOOK

This one was shown to be by my great Uncle Harold who, when a round of drinks was called for was always the first to put his hand into his pocket... and leave it there.

I can't ever remember him buying a round and yet he was the drunkest man I ever knew. What better testimonial to his scam expertise could you wish for? But I do remember him showing me this cunning little stunt. It was the best tenner I ever spent.

Begin by placing a brandy glass on the table and a beer mat on top of it. Then borrow a cigarette (you forgetfully left yours in the machine) and balance it vertically, filter end at the bottom, in the centre of the mat. Finally, place a small coin on top of it.

Conclude the arrangements by finding yourself a punter with more money than sense and making the following wager.

"Here's the problem. And it's worth a tenner if you can solve it. All you have to do is get the coin into the brandy glass. That's the easy bit. The difficult bit is getting it in there without touching the coin or the cigarette or the glass."

"Can you touch the beer mat?" someone will ask. "Absolutely not," you reply, happy that someone has taken the bait. "Just can't touch the coin, ciggie, glass or beer mat. Any takers?"

You make the offer as if it's a party trick but as soon as someone steps forward to take up the challenge you deftly turn the trick into a bet. "In fact, if you can do it, I'll give you a tenner." At that they start to smile. "But if you can't, and I can do it, you owe me a tenner." Let the details of your proposition sink in. Tenner if they can, tenner if they can't but you can.

There's an art to persuading someone to take up a bet like this. You want to engage their minds on the problem, saying, "Anyone got any ideas how it can be done?" Once they are thinking about it, it is only a short step to them thinking about the possibility of winning your tenner. They ignore the fact that they might lose theirs.

"And I'll give you two attempts to do it, because it is tricky. Tenner says you can't. Tenner says I can." It won't be long before you smell the sweet scent of readies in the air as one of the increasingly curious crowd opens their wallet, pulls out a crisp note and, unknown to them, bids it farewell.

THE CATCH

This is a great trick. Another stunt that is worth a tenner to see because everyone who sees it will be sure to try it on some other mug.

Most people, when confronted with this problem, will think back to that old stunt in which the juggler swipes away a tray and makes four eggs land in four glasses. That's good, because this trick doesn't work like that. They're not allowed to touch the beer mat, and even if they slapped the edge of the table really hard, all they'd end up with for their trouble is a sore hand; the coin would land up anywhere but in the glass.

The secret to this little scam is a short sharp blast of air that you direct at the underside of the beer mat. You will have to kneel down to do this and the glass should be positioned near the edge of the table. Blow upwards with a short sharp blast at the underside of the mat and glass. The result is that the mat flies away taking the cigarette with it and the coin drops straight down into the glass.

One of the reasons this works so well is that anyone who has spent the entire evening knocking back pints has usually got very little chance of being able to blow out enough air in a short blast to flip over that beer mat – it's like asking them to blow into a breathlyser without using the tube.

Make sure you've practised this a few times before trying it in front of your peers. And don't be surprised if the man handing over the tenner buys you a drink as well. As I said before, it's a bloody good trick.

14 STICKS AND STONES

THE HOOK

Sticks and stones may break my bones but words will never hurt me. I bet you've heard that said a few times. Well, it's about time to find out if the cliché is true with this next bet. Let me just say, it might be a good idea to have a few of your mates standing close by when you attempt to pull this one off.

Picking on the smallest guy in the group you say, "You're not looking too good today Kev." He'll wonder what you mean. "You just look a bit run down that's all. A bit on the weak side. You feeling alright?"

As you are feeding him the bait you've placed a glass tumbler upside down on the table. And on it you've placed a matchbox. You've taken two of the matches out and these you hand to Kev.

"In fact, you look so weak that I bet that you can't even take these two matches and lift that matchbox from the top of the tumbler."

Having seen you in action before, Kev will be a little suspicious. You lift the matchbox away and then drop it back down, saying, "It's not glued in place or anything."

"Look, take a matchstick in each hand. Now I bet you a tenner that using those matchsticks, you can't lift that matchbox from the top of the tumbler within the next twenty seconds."

Say it again if you have too. Kev might not be a professional body builder but he's sure that even he can manage this one. "Are you ready? I'm going to give you twenty seconds and before the time is up you have to lift the matchbox from the top of the tumbler. Do we have a deal?"

Of course you have a deal. What's more, Kev does manage to lift the matchbox using the two matchsticks and within your twenty second time limit. Unfortunately, as he'll soon find out, it isn't enough to win the bet. He should, as he's about to discover, have payed a bit more attention in class.

THE CATCH

Alas for poor Kev the con is all in the wording. You bet him that he couldn't lift the matchbox from the top of the tumbler. He can't because the tumbler is upside down and the matchbox is actually resting on the bottom, not the top. This might sound stupid but as anyone who has argued with his insurer will know, words are very important when it comes to making a contract. And, as with this stunt, it's always the punter who loses.

The time limit you set on the bet ensures that the punter doesn't have too long to think about it, and also acts as a red herring. He will be busy trying to grab the matchbox between the matchsticks as you count him down from twenty to one. Get everybody to join in, that way, at the conclusion, everyone seems to be on your side and he's slightly less likely to kick up a fuss.

Maybe next time Kev will pay more attention to what you say. And he'll definitely be checking those insurance policies when he gets home.

15 DOWN IN ONE

THE HOOK

They've seen it on television, they've seen it on holiday, and they've probably even seen it down their local. Sometime sooner or later every Jack the lad will try downing a drink in one, whether it's a pint of lager, a yard of ale or a jug of dodgy Sangria. Why does this phenomenon exist? So that you can pull this scam, that's why.

First, set out your stall, asking Bob the Belly, who you know has a throat like an open drain, whether he could down his pint in one. No doubt he will boast of the many fine times he's had impressing the lucky senoritas of Benidorm by doing just that. His mother must be so proud.

Having confirmed your character assessment, you issue the challenge:

"I bet you couldn't drink a pint in thirty seconds." Thirty seconds?! He will laugh at such a thought. And within less time than it takes to belch, he has placed a grubby ten pound note on the table and is looking for you to do the same.

You draw in some spectators to see fair play, and one of them acts as timekeeper. Bob orders a fresh pint and feels so confident that he persuades the barmaid to fill it to the very brim. No head.

"Ready, steady, go!" The bellymeister lifts the pint, tilts it to a well-practised angle and proceeds to drain the contents. He's good. He's very good; a fact that you'll depend upon.

The empty glass is slammed against the bar, a podgy hand wipes across thick wet lips and he asks, "How'd I do?"

"You did fine," says the man with the watch. "Ten seconds dead." Bob is about to reach for the money but he is too late. You are already placing it into your wallet. And the wide-eyed expression on your victim demands an explanation.

THE CATCH

The Belly has been defeated by something he never quite mastered. Words, of the unslurred variety. The bet, as you remind him, was "to drink the pint in thirty seconds." Unfortunately for him, he did it in ten. Not quite the same thing.

Let his protests fall on deaf ears. Possession is nine-tenths of the law: you might not technically have a legal background but you watched a hell of a lot of *Judge Judy* on daytime TV when you were between jobs.

The very best defence you have for dodgy bets is to immediately give the punter a chance to win his money back with another proposition. For some bizarre reason this tends to satisfy honour. It will be equally dubious but he doesn't need to know that. The notion that they might lose a second time hardly enters into it. But then maybe that's not surprising. After all, they didn't think they'd lose the first time round either.

⒗ BOTTLE OPENER

THE HOOK

If you managed to get away with a verbal con of the kind used in *Down in One* then here's one that could earn you a bottle of champagne.

It depends on a friendly barman, a gullible punter and some slick talking. Bob the Belly will see a possibility for revenge when you make the following offer, "I bet I can take a drink out of a bottle of champagne without opening it."

"What bottle of champagne?" asks Bob.

"The one you're going to pay for if I succeed" you reply. You also add that if you fail, the champagne is on you.

Bob will still be licking his wounds from the last bet but he'll ask all the right questions. Are you really not going to open it? Not going to break the neck off the bottle or drill a hole through its side? Don't get into too many details if you can help it. Just repeat the challenge, "I promise I'll take a drink from the bottle without opening it, breaking the seal, removing the cork or damaging the bottle in any way." Sounds fair enough and with a bit of prodding, he'll eventually accept the bet.

As soon as he does, you ask the barman to loan you a bottle of champers. This shouldn't be too difficult because he knows that at the end of the bet one or other of you will be paying for it. As usual, however, it won't be you.

THE CATCH

So how do you take a drink from a sealed bottle of champagne without opening it first? Once again words come to your rescue and lure the unwary into the pit of poverty.

When you get the bottle of champagne, look it over very carefully. This is just to build the tension because everyone there will be wondering how on earth you can rise to this challenge. Pick at the top at little, just enough to get Bob to protest. Then look at the label. Apparently satisfied, you remind everyone of the challenge. "I said I'd take a drink out of this bottle without opening it. And if I can, Bobby here has promised to pay for the champagne. Isn't that right Roberto?" He will admit that it is, thereby sealing the deal and his fate before witnesses.

As soon as he does that, you pick up your pint from the bar and turn the champagne bottle upside-down. You'll notice that, unlike most beer and wine bottles, there is a small concave hollow in its base. Pour some of your pint into this, put the rest of the drink down and then take a swig from the bottom of the bottle. You've met the challenge of taking a drink from the bottle without opening it. You never did say that you would be drinking champagne from it. But you will now.

17 FILL HER UP

THE HOOK

It's not that I don't like paying for drinks. It's just that if I can see a way of getting them for free, I have an irresistible urge to pull a scam. Paul Newman summed it up in the movie, The Colour of Money: "A dollar won is twice as sweet as a dollar earned." Ain't that the truth.

Commonsense tells you that it is not always possible to drink for free but that doesn't mean you need to pay full price either. Take the following; it won't make you a fortune but it will get you drinks at bargain prices.

The proposition is best used early in the evening. That way you establish a pattern and are free to try it on everyone who comes your way. In fact, you'll find that those who you've already unashamedly hustled positively encourage you to pull it on their friends. No one wants to be singled out as stupid and so they find comfort in the humiliation of their peers.

Here is the wager. When your friend arrives, after they've bought themselves a drink, say "I bet you that I can drink your drink, snap my fingers and make it instantly reappear in your glass. And I will swallow it – no spitting it out or any tricks like that, I promise! In fact you can even hold the empty glass. And to make it even more difficult, place this beer mat over the top and hold it down tight so that nothing can get inside."

No one who knows you will want to bet with you, not after you've been working all the stunts in this book. But your mate will still be intrigued. He'll definitely want to see this trick. A glass magically refilling itself? Sounds like the miracle he's always dreamt of. So you make it easy for him to take the wager by saying "It's just for fun. Say fifty pence?"

Well, fifty pence isn't much to lose and you've just got yourself a deal. But how will you make the trick work?

THE CATCH

The answer is that you don't. There is no easy way that you can make a drink reappear in the glass while he's holding it. And you're not going to waste time trying to figure out how you could do it either.

What you are going to do is savour his drink when you take it. And when it fails to reappear in the glass, you hand him your fifty pence. It will be the cheapest drink you'll buy all evening but not the only one because you can pull the same scam on every friend of his that arrives at the bar.

Compare and contrast with the old slap-in-the-face favourite: "I bet you a pound I can make your breasts move without touching them…"

18 CAP IN HAND

THE HOOK

Not everyone will appreciate your wit and verbal dexterity. The thought that you cheated them out of their cash or a drink using simply a few choice phrases could be considered rather underhand. People like Bob the Belly would prefer something more honest. Arm wrestling over broken glass for instance. It's wise therefore to play to what they imagine are their strengths. In this case you challenge Bob to come outside and sort it out man to man. Well, almost.

What you actually say is "I bet I can throw a bottle top further than you. Much further. Ten quid says I can." And as a taster of your Olympian skills you pick up a bottle cap and skim it across the bar.

Like the barman, Bob is not impressed. He's a member of the local rugby club; when he's not knocking back beer he's chasing and hugging other big men with odd-shaped balls.

Pick up another bottle cap and bend it between your fingers, as an open exhibition of brute force. And challenge him again. "What do you say? Ten quid says I can throw a bottle cap further than you can. Are you coming outside or what?"

The thought that everyone might think him too chicken to step outside with you is enough to goad him into action again and another portrait of QE2 is teased from his wallet. Five minutes later you are both standing in the car park with a handful of bottle caps. Each of you is allowed to make a couple of practice throws but it's the third one that will count. Whoever throws their bottle cap furthest wins the contest – that much is fair.

Bob gives it his best shot – the wind blows the cap in a curve but it's a good throw all the same. Seeing this you take off your jacket and start to get serious. You take a short run and then fling your bottle cap into the air. It leaves your hand with amazing speed, going out of the car park, over the road and off into the distance. There's no doubt as to who the winner is.

THE CATCH

This stunt is a version of a favourite of that great U.S. gambler Titanic Thompson, only he did it with walnuts rather than beer bottle caps. He had prepared his walnut beforehand by filling it full of lead shot. The extra weight meant that he could outdistance even a professional sportsman when it came to the throw.

You use the same swindle, but insert a coin into the bottle cap before you throw it. The coin should be as close to the internal diameter of the bottle cap as possible; with some you will be able to just wedge them in place, with others you might need to bend over opposite sides of the cap slightly to grip them. The added weight gives your cap extra momentum, and even with moderate strength you should be able to throw yours considerably further than your opponent. Save this one for the evening. That way no one is likely to find your gaffed bottle cap in the dark.

19 LOT OF BOTTLE

THE HOOK

It was the shape of the bottle that made the bet in *Bottle Opener* possible and so it is with this next proposition. It requires three of the original-style Coca Cola bottles.

You arrange the bottles so that one of them is lying on the table trapped by it's middle between the other two.

Then you take a match and lodge it between the bottles as shown. Although the bottles hold the match in place, the slightest shifting of them will cause the match to fall. With the arrangement complete, you make your bet.

"I'll give ten quid to anyone who can free the centre bottle without the match falling. Problem is that you mustn't touch either of the other bottles, only the centre one. And you can't touch the match. Ten quid says it can be done. Any takers?"

Let your prospective punters study the puzzle from all angles but don't let them touch anything until they've taken your bet. Only he who pays, plays.

Best of all, you will give the challenger two attempts to solve it.

THE CATCH

At first glance it looks impossible. The middle bottle is held locked between the other two. Those who attempt the challenge usually try to move the bottle upwards towards the neck and free it where the gap is widest. But moving the bottle is almost sure to make the match fall. It really doesn't matter whether they have two or three attempts to solve the puzzle; it just won't work that way.

The solution is ingenious and you should only reveal it when you are sure the money is going to be paid over. You pick up the matchbox from which you took the match, and take out a second matchstick. Strike it and use it to set light to the head of the first matchstick. It will flare up immediately and weld itself to the bottle. You can now simply pull the middle bottle free. The outer bottles will separate but the matchstick will not fall.

THE HOOK

This particular scam became popular with conmen around forty years ago where it was played out in bars all over the United States.

This works best with a largish crowd. First you befriend one of the bar staff and ask if you can borrow a ten or twenty pound note from the till, offering to show them an amazing trick. Have them sign the note, "So that you'd recognise it if you ever saw it again" and then fold it up into a small packet. Place the note under a napkin or bar towel and let several people reach under and confirm that it is still there. It is.

Now for the magic. You flick the napkin open and, to everyone's amazement, the note has disappeared. Completely gone. It's not up your sleeves, in the napkin or in your hand. It's gone. Forever.

Well, you could bring it back if you wanted to. And that's when you turn the trick into a bet. "You've just lost ten quid from the till. Must be worth a free drink to get it back? Let's say I make that same ten quid reappear inside the till. Would that be a good trick? Would it be worth a drink?"

Of course it would. Now it's just a matter of getting the barman to shout the magic words "Izzy Wizzy" as loud as he possibly can. And believe me, if he wants to get the money back he will have to shout anything you tell him to. Personally, I make him stand on a bar, put one finger in his ear and roll up a trouser leg as well. But that's the sort of person I am.

Then, lo and behold, he's asked to open up the till and there inside is the note for everyone to see, complete with his signature. What a trick! What a scam more like.

THE CATCH

This is a racket from start to finish. First you need a mate to act as a stooge. He is the last person to feel the note under the handerchief. He doesn't just feel it, he also secretly takes it from you and palms it away. If no one knows he's in on the scam, his actions won't be suspected.

While the attention is on you and the ritual humiliation of the barman, your friend casually wanders away to the other end of the bar, taking the note with him. He then asks one of the other bar staff for change for the cigarette machine, and that's the simple but sneaky way that the signed note ends up back in the till and you end up with a free drink.

As I said before, this trick was used by conmen to swindle bars out of money - they made their profit from the change that is handed over to the stooge. Of course you wouldn't be that dishonest and neither would I – we'd hand the cash back afterwards. Wouldn't we?

A far more more honest and satisfying way of making a few quid on top of your free drink is to make a side bet with someone beforehand: "A tenner says that by the end of the evening that barman will be standing on the bar shouting 'Izzy Wizzy' with a finger in one ear and his trouser leg rolled up."

TWO
TIPPED OFF

"A FOOL AND HIS MONEY WERE
LUCKY TO GET TOGETHER IN
THE FIRST PLACE."
- ANONYMOUS

21 HEADS I WIN, TAILS YOU LOSE

THE HOOK

It's been a cracking meal. And your mate's been good company. Haven't seen him for ages. But this gaff is a bit on the pricey side and you wonder why he picked such a posh restaurant. It's as if along with his new promotion he's become a bit flash. Well, if he can afford his half of the meal, he can afford yours too.

The bill arrives. It's got more numbers on it than a lottery ticket.

"Tell you what, let's toss for it," you say. He agrees and you take out a coin and flip it into the air.

By the time the coin lands, there's a good chance you might be eating for free. But the main thing is there's absolutely no chance that you will be paying for both meals.

THE CATCH

In the old days, a double-headed coin would have done the trick. But most people are wise to that one.

What they probably won't have seen is a coin that has been nicked at the edge with a knife on the tail side so that a tiny 'burr' is projecting.

That's the coin you are using for the bet.

Timing is important on this one so listen up. Take out the coin as though at random from a handful of change as you say,

"Tell you what, let's toss for it." As you already have a coin to hand, he won't offer to supply one himself. Toss the coin up in the air in time-honoured tradition, catch it and slap it on the back of your hand.

"Heads or tails?" you ask. While he thinks

about it, you press the coin against the back of your hand and slide it slightly. If it is heads up, you will feel the tiny projection on the tail side prick your skin. If it is tails up, you won't feel anything. In other words, you now know which call will be right.

If he calls incorrectly, uncover the coin and show him. You've just eaten for free.

If he calls correctly, you can do one of two things depending on how cocky you are feeling. Either smile and say, "No, I can't do it. I was going to trick you but I can't take your money! We'll split the bill," as you put the coin away *without ever looking at it*. He'll think you've just been joking all along.

Or, if you're like me, you'll just flip the coin over towards him with your thumb as you lift your hand away. It's actually very easy to do. Remember, he has no idea that you already know which way up the coin is.

So there you have it. Play the game almost fair and you'll dine for free half the time. Use the thumb swindle and you'll never pay for a meal again. Can't say fairer than that can you?

22 IT'S A DATE

THE HOOK

"There's no point tossing a coin and calling heads or tails is there? There'd be a fifty-fifty chance I'd win, even if I didn't cheat." At least you're vaguely honest with your fellow diner as you make yet another attempt at a free meal. "Let me give you some real odds. Take out any coin from your pocket. Don't look at it and place it on the table. Cover it with your hand so that I can't see it."

"Now then," you say, "I'm prepared to bet you the cost of lunch that I can guess the date. Keep the coin covered. You mustn't let me see it. In fact, if you think I've already seen it, take out another coin and put it on the table."

This bet is definitely too good to refuse. The punter's hand is on the coin. He knows that you don't even know what the coin is so how can you possibly guess the date? Ah, but you can. And that's why you won't be buying lunch.

THE CATCH

If your victim had drank less he might have listened more carefully. You never said that you'd tell him the date on the coin. What you said was that you would tell him the date. And so you do – today's date!

The bet can be played as a competition. You invite the punter to take out a coin and cover it. You then say, "Whoever guesses closest to the correct date, gets a free lunch. The other one wins the coin and adds it to the money he'll need to pay the bill." No matter what he calls, you once again call out today's date leaving him with a hefty bill.

One more tip that might occasionally come in useful in situations like this. As you can imagine, it can sometimes be difficult to get someone to pay out when you've just swindled them in such a basic way. But, if the punter is a bloke, one thing's for sure: he's unlikely to want to look like a bad loser in front of the waitress or barmaid he's been ogling all night. So get her to hold your credit cards or cash until the bet's been settled. Having spent the entire meal drooling over her every move, he'll do anything to avoid looking like a cheapskate.

23 TIME IS MONEY

THE HOOK

The average punter's powers of observation are not at their best after a wine-soaked meal. Which is just as well, because this bet depends on that fact.

You begin by asking your dining companion about his watch; how long has he had it, where did he buy it, how much did it cost him? General questions of no particular significance it might seem. Then you make the following proposition: "I'm going to ask you three questions about your watch. They are easy questions. If you get them all right, I'll buy dinner. If you get any of them wrong, dinner's on you. Now before we start, let me say that the questions are really very simple. So easy that, if you don't agree that you should know the answers, we'll call the whole bet off."

If he decides to take the bet – and having answered your first questions without any problem he'd be hard pressed not to - then you've just enjoyed that meal for free.

THE CATCH

It is amazing how many times this scam works. People are amazingly poor observers when it comes to even the most personal of possessions and when put on the spot find themselves unable to recall even the simplest details. The only restriction with this wager is that you can only use it with punters who are wearing a traditional watch as opposed to a digital one. Well, unless they are completely legless, but where's the challenge in that?

Here are the questions:

 Without looking, does your watch have a second hand? More than likely he will get this one right. Let him answer and then move on to the next question.

 Again without looking, does your watch have a number 6 on it? This is quite tricky. He probably won't remember whether the watch has Roman or Arabic numerals. And many watches don't have any numbers at all; just lines at the 3, 6, 9 and 12 hour positions, if anything at all. When he's answered, ask him to check his watch and let you know if he was correct.

 Finally, and this is the killer, ask him what time it is – without looking at his watch again. Despite the fact that he just looked at it a few seconds ago, the chances are that he never noted the time.

If you're in any doubt about whether that's likely to be the case, try asking someone the time and then ask them the same question again just moments later and see whether or not they can answer you correctly without having another look.

 WORTH A PACKET

THE HOOK

Ever got caught by one of those fake auctions or 'run outs' where they promise to sell you a television, a DVD player and a dishwasher, all for a fiver, and when you get back home you find that what you've actually bought is a set of plastic spanners? Well, you'll find the same auction fever at work here.

It begins simply enough. You ask one of your dining compadres for twenty quid, enough to cover your share of the meal you've just had. If he has any sense, he'll say no. But you persuade him to play your game by offering up twenty quid of your own. Fold it up and stick it in an empty cigarette packet. Having put your own money down, ask for his, saying, "Come on, twenty quid, I'm about to make you an offer you can't refuse."

Take his twenty, fold it up and put it in the cigarette packet with yours. Hold the box up and give it a shake, saying, "There's forty quid inside here. Have I taken anything out of the box since we began?" He'll have to agree that you haven't. You've been careful to let him see your hands empty all the time you've been handling the money.

"In that case, would you give me fifty quid for this packet and its contents?" Of course he wouldn't. "How about forty?" Still not exactly a bargain; all he'd be gaining is the cigarette packet. "Well how about if I offered to sell you the lot for thirty quid?" He considers the offer and eventually agrees. Who wouldn't?

THE CATCH

The truth is that if he gives you thirty quid for the forty in the fag packet, he's actually buying back twenty quid of his own, therefore losing out to the tune of ten smackers...think about it.

25 NUMBERS UP

THE HOOK

One of the secrets of a good proposition bet is luring the victim into a situation that makes it comfortable for them to risk money. That means getting the money from his wallet and onto the table without arousing suspicion. So it's always good to start with a puzzle or a bit of trivia. For instance:

"Do you know what the most commonly used letter in the England language is?" He might or might not but the answer, as you inform him, is the letter E. Fascinating. Now you take it one stage further. "Do you know what the most commonly used digits from 0 to 9 are?"

Let him guess three digits and whatever he says agree with him. "2, 5, and 7? That's absolutely right. That's amazing; you've obviously got a lucky streak. In fact I bet that if you took out a ten pound note from your wallet, you'd find at least two of these digits in the serial number."

Take out a tenner of your own, and place it on the table, saying, "And if there isn't, you can have my tenner. On the other hand, if there is, I get to keep yours."

THE CATCH

There are eight digits in the serial number on a banknote, any of which could obviously be one of the numbers that your punter calls. They can choose any three digits so long as they are different. The odds are heavily in your favour on this one but you will still sometimes lose, so on that basis you might want to play it with everyone you meet. Who needs friends anyway?

 THE WEIGH-IN

THE HOOK

"I'm going to ask you some simple questions. If you manage to get them all right, I'll pay for lunch. If you get one wrong, you pay for lunch."

It is, of course, another one of your justly famous 'can't lose' propositions. And it all appears to be done purely in the name of fun. Of course it does. As you issue the challenge you arrange several small objects from your pockets on the table. You need a packet of cigarettes (preferably empty or thereabouts), a small coin and a cigarette lighter. Line them up in a row just in front of the punter.

"Are you ready?" You don't wait to see whether he wants to play or not – that should never be an option. It is entirely up to him to say no. By not saying anything, he is becoming party to the bet – it's as good as a contract – especially if you have other people at the table watching what you are doing. Never underestimate the power of peer pressure.

"Okay, now listen carefully. I'm going to ask you to pick up two objects at a time. Then I'll ask you a question about them. And there will be three questions in all. Understand?"

His "yes" to understanding what the bet is about will be taken by everyone else to also be a "yes" to accepting the bet itself, which you now repeat in case anyone is in any doubt. "If you get all three questions right, I'll pay for your meal. If you get one wrong, you pay for mine. Okay?" His grunt can also be taken as acknowledgement of his willing participation.

And then you go straight into the questions. Need I say that he won't get them all correct?

THE CATCH

The objects on the table are not as randomly chosen as they appear. For the first question you point to the cigarette packet and the coin and ask him to pick them up, one in each hand. Then you say, "Which is the biggest one?"

He'll say the packet of cigarettes, which is obviously the right answer, and you tell him to put them down. Note that you only ever point to the objects. You never ever name them.

Now, point to the cigarette packet and the lighter and ask him to pick them up. Ask him, "Which one is the heavier?" He'll say it is the cigarette lighter. Correct again. Ask him to put them down.

Finally, get him to pick up the coin in one hand and the cigarette lighter in the other and ask him, "Which is the lighter?" Amazing as it may seem, he will nominate the five pence piece because he has been thinking in terms of size and weight. To your own selfish and devious ends you point to the cigarette lighter and say, "No, that's the lighter; that's the coin."

Another free lunch to you.

27 COINING IT IN

THE HOOK

It's a well know fact that after a few bevvies the brain's powers of observation and logic go into a steady decline. Perversely though, and fortunately for us, El Vino convinces even the most sensible that their powers of perception have been enhanced beyond measure.

The following bet exploits your punter's alcohol-induced infallibility. Which is just as well because you've been reduced to raiding the piggy bank for this one. You will need a lot of coins, all the same value. Let's assume that your total worth at this point in time can be summed up with a handful of two-pence pieces.

Arrange them on the table in small piles. The first pile consists of a single coin. The second pile has five coins. The third eight coins, the fourth ten coins and the fifth thirteen coins. Five piles of coins, arranged in a row as shown.

Keep one coin on display as you make your wager. "Which of these piles of coins do you think is as high as the coin is wide?"

You might have to speak slowly to make sure you are understood. So say it again if you have too, expanding on the premise so that it is clear even to the dullest. "Which pile of coins is the same height as this coin is wide?" Hold up the coin for him to see and then place it away in your pocket.

To give his choice an edge, you wager the price of the meal on him being unable to choose the right pile. It seems a simple bet but more often than not, your victim will be wrong.

THE CATCH

This is a cunning optical illusion and you will need to try it with some coins to fully appreciate how effective it is. In the case of the two-pence piece, most people will pick the fourth pile of coins. Ten coins seem more than ample to equal the diameter of a two-pence piece. But they'd be wrong. The correct pile is the last one, containing thirteen coins and you prove this by taking out another two-pence and standing it on end beside it.

The trick works with any circular coin. Just make sure that you leave enough space between the piles to further confuse the eye.

MATCH POINT

THE HOOK

There's nothing like a friendly after-dinner game to sort out who should pay the bill. And that's what this is; nothing like a friendly game.

You take out a box of matches, which you just happen to have with you, and tip the contents into an ashtray. The game is simple. You and the punter each take a number of matches from the ashtray alternately. Whoever takes the last match is the winner. The loser buys lunch.

There is only one rule: each time you reach into the ashtray you can only take up to three matches. One, two or three, that's it. But because the punter hasn't played this game before, you give him the advantage of taking the first turn — you're a charitable kind of guy.

He reaches in and takes some matches. You do the same. And you continue this until one of you wins the game by taking the last match from the ashtray. Naturally, it will be you.

THE CATCH

The game is rigged from the start. You know exactly how many matches are in the matchbox. It doesn't have to be any precise number though, as long as it is divisible by four. I find that thirty-two or thirty-six matches make for a good game.

Let the punter take the first turn and watch how many matches he takes. Then, when you take your turn, take enough matches to make his number up to four. For example, if he takes one match, you take three. If he takes two matches, you also take two. Every time he takes matches you take enough to make it up to the magical number four.

If you are mathematically minded, you can probably see where this is leading. At the end of the game there will be four matches left in the ashtray, but since he can only take up to three matches, it leaves you with the last one. And it leaves him with the lunch bill.

Incidentally, there's an additional twist on this. Start by demonstrating the game, telling him that the object is for each of you to remove up to three matches at a time. Once he understands that, ask him whether he would like to take the first or the second turn. If he chooses to go first, you announce that whoever takes the last match is the winner. If he chooses to go second, tell him that whoever takes the last match is the loser. Either way, using the same principle as above, you can always manoeuvre him into a losing position.

29 GAME, SET AND MATCH

THE HOOK

Believe it or not, quite often you can earn yourself a little extra cash by simply explaining how you conned your victim in the first place. *Match Point* is a good example. Having won the bet and ensured that the loser paid the bill, you can later offer to share the secret of your success, for a price. It may be a drink at the bar or much more. It all depends on how desperate your victim is to know and how good your negotiating skills are.

A price having been set, you then explain the trick; how when he took his turn you observed the number of matches he removed and simply did a little addition to work out how many matches you should take. Pour some matches into the ashtray and let him practise a little. He will soon get the hang of it. And when he has, you make him another little wager. In fact you confess to feeling a bit guilty that you swindled a good lunch out of him.

"How about we play a game for a tenner? This time I'll go first."

Like a lamb at a butchers convention, he quickly agrees and the game begins. And yet, although he follows your strategy exactly, he still manages to lose. Pity that, because as soon as you've got your hands on his tenner, you suddenly remember a previous appointment. Got to run.

THE CATCH

Turning a crooked game into an even more crooked game is a favourite ruse of professional cheats. There is no-one as easily deceived as someone who's got his heart set on cheating someone else. So watch out.

The trick is simple but needs to be executed with an air of nonchalance. You take the first turn and play the strategy you have outlined. You proceed in this way until about half the matches have been taken. Next time it is your turn, take out some matches and place them on the table. However, don't place them all on the table. Keep just one hidden in your fingers. Next time you take your turn, drop the hidden match into the ashtray as you dip into it. The punter won't spot this. Take your turn as usual and let him count how many matches you have removed.

Because of the extra match, the victim's entire strategy has been spoiled. Instead of four matches in the ashtray near the end of the game, there will be five. And if you play the finish correctly, you can always leave him with the last match and walk away with his tenner.

Another good way to use this swindle is to persuade him to use it on one of your mates. What he doesn't realise is that your pal also knows about secretly putting a match back into the ashtray.

My own personal tactic is to offer to hold the money while the two of them play. Halfway through I'm 'unexpectedly' called to the phone – that way I can't be held responsible if our chump messes up and loses.

You can split the winnings with your mate later.

THE HOOK

In this scam you don't just win one meal, you win two. Imagine the scene; you and a couple of mates, Gazza and Dave, out for a curry, ordering without bothering to look at the prices on the menu because you know that although a hefty bill will be coming your way, you won't be paying it. Not that you are stingy – much. Divided between the three of you it wouldn't break the bank, but how much better if Dave, who quite frankly came along uninvited and you've never liked him anyway, was to pay all of it?

Before the bill arrives, and therefore before Dave can discover the true scale of his potential losses, you explain a little dinner ritual that you and Gazza have had for years. Rather than deal with all that complicated long division and trying to figure out who had what, you just toss a match and whoever loses pays the bill. You demonstrate by taking the book of matches from the ashtray and tearing one out. You mark one side of the match with an X. The other side is marked with a O. Then you toss the match and let it fall on the table. It is just a variation on tossing a coin and calling heads or tails.

Since Dave has made it a ménage a trois, this complicates things a bit. Or so you say. Then you have an idea.

"I'll tell you what Dave, as it's your first time here, we'll let you off easy. If it comes down X side up, I'll pay. If it comes down O side up, Gazza pays. And if it lands on it's edge, you pay!"

Give a laugh as you make the bet, as if the chances of a paper match landing on its edge were more remote than winning the lottery without buying a ticket. Gazza plays the innocent, laughs too and says "Why not?" forcing Dave to agree, after all, it looks like he's in for a free meal. However, as you've probably learned by now, things are not quite as they seem and it'll be a long time before Davey boy cramps the lads' style again.

THE CATCH

Not much to explain on this one. It takes a lot of practise to toss a paper match so that it lands on its edge, but you can help it out by bending it into an 'L' shape just before you throw it.

As you swing your hand upwards to make the toss, lay the match across

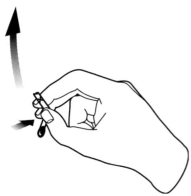

your fingers and push against its centre with your thumbnail. It will crease instantly and, much to Dave's surprise and irritation, will come down to land on its edge.

31 FOUR PLAY

THE HOOK

A book of matches offers a surprising number of possibilities for extracting cash from the unwary. Here's one of my favourites. I like it because there's no chance of the punter deciding not to play. The money is gone before he even suspects that he's put it at risk.

It's Friday night, much alcohol has been consumed and dinner was great. If only it didn't cost so much. Time to start defraying your expenses by picking out a likely looking individual and involving him in a little party game. Tell him you'll show him a trick and ask him for the loan of a tenner. People never loan money to strangers but they seem happy to hand it and other valuables freely to magicians knowing full well that it will come to harm. It's something I've never understood but I'm grateful that they do.

Place the tenner in the centre of the table. Make a big deal of straightening the note out so that it's absolutely flat. And if you can't iron all the wrinkles out of it, ask for a crisper note. The idea is to take the victim's mind far away from any thought that he might be about to lose his money. Bear in mind that if you are using the scams in this book, your reputation might well have preceded you. Some people are going to be cautious about handing over their hard-earned dosh.

Take out a matchbook, tear out four matches and arrange them around the note, one on each of the four sides. Again, make a big deal of setting the matches exactly parallel with the sides of the note. This is all bluff and bluster and has nothing to do with the scam.

With everything set, say "I bet you a quid that you won't answer 'four matches' to every question I ask. And I'm going to ask four questions only, one for each match."

A quid isn't much to lose and so it's a miserable geezer that won't play along. On the other hand, he'll regret it the moment he does.

THE CATCH

These are the questions you ask: "What is your name?" He will answer "Four matches" and you give him one of the matches from the table.

"Where do you live?" Again he answers "Four matches" and you give him another one.

"What's this on the table?" You say, pointing to the tenner. He answers as before and gets his third match in return.

"What will you take for this tenner?" And this is crunch time. If he isn't thinking (and most people aren't), he will say, "four matches," at which point you hand him the fourth match and pocket the tenner.

And if he doesn't fall for that, you've still won the quid from your original bet. All you have to do now is go find nine other mugs.

32 CUP WINNER

THE HOOK

You've got to know what you are doing when working this one but done casually it can be a winner. You hand a matchbook to your punter and ask him to take out a bunch of matches, tear them in half and drop them into an empty coffee cup. You are doing the same with a second book of matches; tearing some matches out, breaking them in half and dropping them into the same cup as him. After you've done this with a dozen or so matches, put your matchbook aside and ask him to do the same. So far, so fair.

No-one knows how many bits of match are in the cup and so it seems like a reasonable bet when you propose that each of you alternately reach in and take out a piece until the cup is empty. Whoever takes the last piece, pays for the meal. The proposition is anything but reasonable. Even though you've no idea how many matches are in the cup you're certain that you'll win.

THE CATCH

No matter how many matches are torn from the matchbooks, there will always be an even number of pieces in the cup as you broke them all into two. So if you take your turn first, your victim will always be left with the last piece.

In the cold light of day the ruse seems absurd but in my experience people rarely think so clearly the night before, especially if they are having a good time. Which they will be until the bill arrives.

If you're feeling generous, you can offer your opponent a 'rematch', this time offering to let him take the first piece from the cup. Of course, what he doesn't know is that when you tore your matches in half you didn't put all pieces in the cup. You secretly kept one back. With an odd number of pieces in play, once again he will lose.

🂭🂭 MATCHBOX MONTE

THE HOOK

It's said that the best way to make a small fortune is to start with a big one. That's also true of anyone who's happy to throw their money at the monte men that work the streets of most major European cities. Whether they are throwing around three cards and asking you to 'find the lady' or manipulating three walnut shells and a pea, the outcome is always the same: you lose. But in this game you're the winner, because now you're playing the role of the monte man and your dinner companion plays the part of the sucker.

You ask the waiter for three boxes of matches and, obligingly, he brings them. You tip out the matches from the boxes so that they're all empty. Then, hiding them underneath the table, you refill one of them with matches. The question is, which one?

You lay the three boxes in a row on the table, mix them around and ask the punter to point to whichever one he thinks contains the matches. If he has any sense, he will tell you that it's impossible to know – how could he? He's right, so you demonstrate which one it is by picking up one of the boxes and rattling it before putting it down again. "Okay, let's start again. I'm going to mix the boxes up and all you have to do is keep your eye on the one that's full."

Slowly you mix the boxes up, moving them one at a time around the table. Then you ask him again which box contains the matches. He immediately points to one and this time he's correct. Now you turn up the heat. "Good. Let's play it again and this time, if you get the right box, I'll pay for the meal. But if you guess wrong, dinner's on you, okay?"

He thinks the game is easy, which is a shame because as soon as the game turns into a bet he has absolutely no chance of picking out the right box.

THE CATCH

What your friend across the table doesn't know is that you have a fourth matchbox hidden up your right sleeve. It contains a few matches and is held against your arm by an elastic band. You hid it there on your last visit to the loo.

When you load matches into one of the boxes, make sure you know which one it is. You might want to mark it by running your thumbnail across the top. This is because the first part of the game is played fairly. You mix the boxes up and ask the punter to guess which one contains the matches. As he didn't see which box you put them into, he'll probably complain about how unfair the game is. That's when you pick up one of the empty matchboxes with the right hand and give it a shake. The punter will hear the matches rattling in the box strapped to your forearm and will assume that the empty box in your hand is actually full. Put this box down on the table and begin the second phase of the game.

Move the boxes around slowly, making sure that the punter is following the empty matchbox. That's the box he'll point to at the finish. Again, pick it up with the right hand and give it a quick shake. The punter hears the matches rattle around and congratulates himself on his powers of observation.

Having got him interested you make the wager and mix the boxes around for the third time. The punter is still following the empty box and at the end of the game will be absolutely amazed when he finds that his wallet is just as empty.

34 DROPPING THE CHARGES

THE HOOK

"Do you believe in hypnotism?" you ask the punter. "Because I bet I can hypnotise you. I'm sure I can. You look the type." Now no-one likes to look like "the type", so they'll ask what you mean. "You look suggestible," you reply. "In fact, I'm prepared to bet dinner on it." The stage is set for a demonstration of bogus hypnosis that will hopefully land you a real meal.

THE CATCH

You show him what to do by placing your hands together palm to palm, as if in prayer. Rest your elbows on the table. Ask him to do as you do and follow your actions precisely. As he does, you tell him to spread out his fingers.

Next, tell him to bend his middle fingers inwards so that they cross. Finally, pick up the bill, fold it and slide it between his extended third fingers.

So far he won't feel anything other than uncomfortable, but it's now that the bet really begins.

"You've got to keep your hands tight together. Keep hold of the bill. Keep your middle fingers bent. That's important; you *really* don't want to separate your hands. Keep your thumbs together. Understand?"

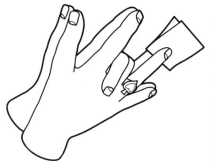

He'll understand. Now you start your hypnotic jiggery pokery. "I want you to count backwards from ten to one, and as you count, the fingers of your hand will grow numb and will start to lose their feeling. So much so that when I snap my fingers you won't be able to drop the bill onto the table without moving your *other* fingers. That's the only way you will be able to drop the bill. Are you ready?"

Get them to count slowly "ten, nine, eight, seven," and so on. When they get to "one" snap your fingers and say "The bill is yours. The bill is yours. The bill *is* yours." He can shake his hands around as much as he likes but no matter how hard he tries he won't be able to release the bill from between his fingers without pulling his hands apart or making some other digital adjustment. It has nothing to do with hypnosis though; it's just another top swindle. The bill really is his though.

⑨⑤ A RIGHT HANDFUL

THE HOOK

"How about we arm wrestle for the meal? No, just kidding. Don't want to cause a scene." You are preparing the way for an interesting little wager. "Besides, you're bigger than me. Probably break my arm." You are in fact just basting the turkey a little before serving him up. "But I'm willing to bet you this. That there's something here, right now, that you can lift with your right hand but not with your left."

It sounds dodgy and you won't want to say this too loudly otherwise you'll get some very funny looks from the other tables. But you do want to get out of paying for this meal so you go over it again, quietly "I can see that your left hand is a bit weak. So as I say, I think there is something right here, in plain sight, that you can lift with your right hand but you'd have trouble holding in your left hand. In fact I'm so sure you that can't pick it up with your left hand that I'll bet the price of dinner on it."

Look at the array of objects on the table as you speak, implying that the object in question might be an empty wine bottle, a coffee cup or a plate. And wait for curiosity to get the better of him.

THE CATCH

With the bet accepted you ask him to hold out both hands. Then you push his left hand upwards while holding his right hand, palm upwards, at table height. Repeat the wager, "I bet the price of dinner that there is something you can lift with your right hand but can't with your left"... and then bring his right palm up to his left elbow.

He can lift his left elbow in his right hand, but he'll never be able to hold it with his left hand. Ignore the people on the other tables who are staring at you and your elbow-fondling friend; there are other restaurants you can go to next time.

36 CATCH OF THE DAY

THE HOOK

When you went to the fish restaurant you never thought you'd end the meal with an angling competition but that's what you do in this next scam.

The waiter brings over two glasses of water and floating in each of them is an ice cube. "Imagine that's a fish," you say, "and this is your line." The line is nothing more than a length of cotton, which you just happened to have with you. You snap it in two, take half yourself and hand the other half to the punter.

"Here's the game." Describing it as a game takes the heat out of the situation. People like games; they're not so keen on cons. "You've got to use the thread to fish the ice out of the glass. First one to do it is the winner. You can't touch the glass, the water or the ice. That's the rule."

What a wonderfully stupid game, thinks the punter. And just as he is thinking that, you add a rider to the rules, "Loser pays the bill. Winner gets a free meal." Now this might seem a bit harsh so you pacify the punter by adding, "But you have to pull the ice out of the glass in less than sixty seconds to win. Do you want to try first? You just lower the thread in like this."

You give a demonstration, taking your thread between your hands and lowering the centre into the glass where you attempt, unsuccessfully to loop it round the ice cube. It won't take long for the punter to work out that this is a difficult game. And after he has given it a try himself, he'll have no doubt that it's impossible to get the ice out of the glass in under sixty seconds. And so, bizarrely, the bet is on and you've just landed yourself a fish supper.

THE CATCH

A little chicanery is used here. It's virtually impossible to drag the ice out of the glass using the thread. At least I've never managed to do it. Not without cheating.

The cheat consists of some salt, which you have hidden in your hand. Earlier in the meal, when the punter wasn't looking, you grabbed the saltcellar and poured some of its contents into a small heap on your lap. You might have to sneak the top off to do this properly.

While he is practising looping his thread you lower your thread onto the ice in your glass.

Then secretly bring up a pinch of salt and drop it on top of the ice cube and thread. All this is done while your punter is concentrating on his own fishing tackle. The salt melts the ice, which quickly refreezes around the thread, welding it to the cube. Pretend that you are practising too for a while, then officially start the competition. All you have to do is pull on the thread carefully and you will be able to lift the ice cube right out of the water. He's been caught hook, line and sinker.

37 THE FINAL STRAW

THE HOOK

To do this one well, you've got to lead your punter down the garden path and then bolt the gate behind you before he can figure out a way back.

You place two ten-pence pieces on the table and a smaller coin, say a five-pence piece, between them. Then you set a pint glass of soda water on top of it. The glass is full and there is a straw in it. Here's the set-up.

"How long do you think it would take you to drink that glass of soda water?" Doesn't really matter what he answers because you now tell him, "Well, here's a challenge. See that five-pence piece sitting under the glass? I bet I can get it from under the glass faster than you can. Now obviously you're probably thinking that the fastest way of getting the coin is to move the glass. Well, the rule is that you can't move the glass until it's empty. And you can't touch the glass or the coins either. So how fast do you think you can get the coin?"

Whatever he says, offer to bet him the meal that you can do it quicker. You even give him an opportunity to go first. And, if you've led him down the right garden path, he'll start drinking the soda water through the straw so that he can then move the glass according to the rules. Time him on your watch, congratulate him and then show that there's an even faster way.

THE CATCH

The trick is that drinking the pint of soda water through a straw is not the quickest way to get at the coin. There is another way, although it only succeeds if you are working on a tablecloth.

The trick is to scratch at the tablecloth just to one side of the glass, between the two larger coins. Strangely, this sets the coin in motion and if you keep scratching it will slowly crawl towards you and out from under the glass. Easy really. And you don't feel bloated afterwards.

38 TOSS UP

THE HOOK

Here's one for the brave. It isn't a bet you'll win every time but you'll certainly be quids in in the long run. It depends on the laws of probability, those unwritten rules that have caught many a gambler who thought he could pull Lady Luck.

Ask your punter what the odds are of heads coming up if you toss a coin. He should answer fifty-fifty, which is correct. Then ask him how many times heads would come up if you tossed a coin ten times. Doesn't take a genius to figure out that the answer must be five.

"Well, that's interesting. Because I bet you that if you toss a coin ten times, you won't get five heads." Let him think about it, and then make him a wager he can't refuse.

THE CATCH

While he might toss five heads and five tails, he might also toss one head and nine tails, two heads and eight tails, three heads and – well, you get the idea. There are far more combinations possible in ten trials than the one he thinks most probable. The true situation is that the odds of anything other than five heads being tossed are five to two in your favour. Play this strategy over a long run and you should see a substantial profit.

39 IT'S A CORKER

THE HOOK

An empty wine bottle usually means that the evening is at an end. But for you it's the opening of a new gambit by which a little extra pocket money can be earned.

You take the cork that came out of the bottle and push it back inside. It takes some effort, that much is clear from the way you are struggling. First you force it into the neck of the bottle as far as you can and then you take a spoon and use the handle to force the cork all the way down the neck and inside. There's the cork, bouncing around inside the bottle. So far, so good.

Hand the bottle around and ask if anyone can get the cork out without smashing the bottle or breaking the cork. They'll shake the bottle upside down in the feeble hope that the cork will somehow drop out. But it won't. It's there for keeps, or at least that's how it looks.

"I bet you that I can get that cork out. And I won't damage the cork or the bottle. A tenner says I can do it." It seems impossible but it isn't. It isn't free either. If they want to know how it's done, they are going to have to cough up the compulsory ten sovs. But it's worth it – the applause you'll get for accomplishing this cunning stunt is almost as satisfying as the tenner you are about to win. Almost.

THE CATCH

This is one of those rare bets in which you really can make good on your promise. No tricks, no fancy phrases, no underhand manoeuvres. To make it work you need a thin cloth napkin or, better still, silk scarf. So the time to work the bet is when one of your dinner companions is wearing the appropriate fashion accessory.

You borrow the scarf and work a corner of it into the bottle. Push more and more of the scarf inside until only a handful remains outside. Now shake the bottle around until you can maneouvre the cork onto the scarf.

What you do next is something you just won't think possible until you give it a try.

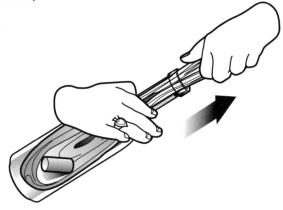

Pull on the scarf, entangling the cork and drawing it nearer to the neck of the bottle. The narrow end of the cork should be in direct line with the opening in the bottle; you'll probably need to jiggle everything around for a while to get into this position. Now give the scarf one almighty tug. At first the cork will jam in the neck of the bottle, but another long hard pull will free it. Make sure nobody is standing to the side of you, sometimes the cork flies out like... well, like a cork from a bottle!

40 HOLEY SMOKE

THE HOOK

I love this. It's a game the punter cannot win and it has a spectacular finale. You introduce it by saying it's an old army game that your grandad showed you. You take a square of tissue paper, torn from a napkin, place it over the mouth of a glass and fasten it in place with an elastic band. And on top of the tissue paper you place a coin.

The game is simple. Each of you takes turns in using a lit cigarette to burn a hole in the tissue paper. As more and more holes are burned into the paper, the coin becomes in danger of falling into the glass. Whoever makes the coin drop, is the loser. It's like a low-tech version of 'Kerplunk'.

It's actually a bloody good game and requires a bit of skill and concentration. Not that any of it will help the punter when you offer to bet the cost of the meal on the next game of *Holey Smoke*.

THE CATCH

This is the only bet in the book that you will need to get a special 'something' for. It's a special kind of tissue paper called "Flash Paper" and you can buy it in magic and joke shops. The paper has a special property; it flares up with a bright flash as soon as you touch it with a lit cigarette and vanishes instantly, almost without trace.

By now you should be ahead of me. After a couple of kosher games using ordinary tissue, you make the bet and place your sheet of flash paper across the top of the glass, holding it in place with the elastic band. All you have to do is let the punter take the first turn. As soon as he touches it with his cigarette, the paper disappears in a flash and the coin drops straight into the glass. Play this in front of a big crowd and not only will you get the tenner, but a huge belly laugh as well.

THREE
SPORTING CHANCE

"DEPEND ON THE RABBITS FOOT
IF YOU WILL, BUT REMEMBER IT
DIDN'T WORK FOR THE RABBIT."
- R.E. SHAW

41 JIGGERY POKERY

THE HOOK

Who wouldn't like to deal like a demon when it comes to playing cards? A real sharp takes years to develop his craft. Fortunately for you there's a quicker way to your opponent's wallet if you follow this crash course in cardsmanship. How about beating your victim's money out of him even after you've let him pick out his own hand? The proposition goes like this:

You bet the punter that you can beat him in a game of poker even if you both choose your hands out of a face-up deck. What's more, you'll let him see which cards you pick so that he has a chance to change his hand for a better one. He won't believe you so you spell it out.

"I'll pick five cards - face up. And then you pick five cards. After that we can both discard and draw more cards to make a better hand, just like ordinary poker. Only one rule: all royal flushes are equal. In other words no suit is better than another. Other than that, the wager is that I won't lose or draw. I'll win."

The bit about the suits being equal appears to mean that he could equal your hand no matter what you picked. If you have a royal flush, he can also pick a royal flush. Couldn't be clearer. Could it?

THE CATCH

Here's the swindle. Spread the cards across the table and let him get a good look at them. Encourage him to think about his strategy before choosing. And remind him that he's to pick out five cards to make up a poker hand, but, as you said before, you'll choose first so that he can evaluate your cards.

You open the game by picking out the four tens and any other card. Make it a two spot or something low. It'll confuse the hell out of him.

Now it's the punter's turn to choose. If he hasn't already spotted it, he will now realise that whatever winning strategy he had contemplated lies in ruins. Since you have all the tens, he can't draw himself the coveted royal flush. Best hand he can make is four aces. Let him take any five cards he likes.

Remind him you said you'd both draw cards again to see if you could better your hands. This time you discard three of the ten spots and the odd card, leaving you just the ten. Draw to it whatever cards necessary to make the highest flush possible. If he holds all the aces, you'll probably end up making a king-high flush.

This strategy, drawing to make the highest flush, will work no matter which cards he holds. And because the tens you had are now in the discard pile and can't be touched by the punter, he can never equal it. This makes you a winner and you didn't even have to deal from the bottom of the deck.

42 POKER IN THE EYE

SPORTING CHANCE

THE HOOK

Maybe letting him select his own cards from the deck in *Jiggery Pokery* was just too much for your punter. Too much choice confused his already over-strained brain. So to make things simple you take out just ten cards from the deck.

"I've got ten cards. I'm going to show them to you one at a time and let you pick five. Whichever five are left, those are the ones I'll have for my hand. Couldn't be fairer – you pick five and I have the leftovers. And yet I'm going to bet that, once again, I'll neither lose nor draw. I'll win."

If it got any simpler you'd be reading him bedtime stories. Who could refuse such a bet? He picks five, leaves you with the rest. Only a foolish man would look a gift horse in the mouth. And yet, if he'd looked closely, he'd probably see you smiling.

THE CATCH

No one ever lost money betting on the greed of others and this devious wager depends on your punter imagining that he smells a free lunch.

The ten cards you remove from the deck are: three tens, three eights, three twos and the ace of spades. Apart from the ace, the other cards can be from any suit

Don't let the punter see which ten cards you're removing from the deck. Shuffle them up a bit, fan them in front of you and cut the packet to bring the ace of spades to round about the third or fourth card from the top. You can do all this as you describe the wager to the victim.

Then drop the packet of ten cards face down onto the table. Once the bet has been accepted, hold up the top card of the packet, show it to him and ask, "Do you want this card or should I have it?" If he wants it, deal it to him. If he thinks you should have it, deal it to yourself.

Go though the entire packet like this, one card at a time until he has five cards. You take the rest. Here's where greed comes in, because as soon as he sees that ace of spades he'll take it. After all it is the highest card in the packet and he's not going to give it to you. Which is a pity because it's the Jonah card of the group. Whoever has that card will lose. And if he takes it, it means you'll always beat him with a full house or two pairs. Try it and see.

43 POKER IN BOTH EYES

THE HOOK

Unlucky punters, in other words anyone who has ever accepted one of your wagers, often demand a rematch. In this case you appear to repeat the bet except the conditions are even fairer than before.

This time you give the punter the ten cards. He shuffles them up to his heart's content and then drops them back on top of the deck. He deals them out, one to you, one to him, until you have five cards each. Well, this time he only has himself to blame. He shuffled. He dealt. He lost.

THE CATCH

When you take the deck, note which card is on top. Let's say it's a four spot. Now take out any other nine cards made up of three banks of three but not including any fours. For instance, three tens, three twos, three Jacks. Doesn't matter what they are as long as none of them are the same value as the top card. And don't let the punter see their faces.

As you do this, casually say: "I'm going to take out ten cards and we'll use them to play poker." This is a lie. There are only nine cards but no-one will question the statement, especially if they've seen you work the *Jiggery Pokery* stunt.

Give the packet of cards to the punter and ask him to shuffle them. When he's finished, ask him to drop the packet face down on top of the deck you are holding. Then place the deck on the table. Here's the bet:

"You've shuffled and now you're going to deal. One to me, one to you. Yet I'm prepared to bet a tenner that I win."

He will be at a loss to see how. But if he deals to you first, as convention dictates, it means that he'll get the four-spot that was originally on top of the deck. This Jonah card will make him the loser and you the winner. Serves him right. He should know better by now.

There's one final twist on this bizarre poker game. If you mark the back of the Jonah card so that you can spot it, you can ask him to pick the ten cards up and give them another shuffle. When he's finished shuffling ask him to deal the cards out into two hands. As he deals, note which hand the marked cards falls to. Now ask him to pick a hand. If he picks the one with the marked card, bet him that you'll win. However, if he picks the other hand, bet him that this time he'll win. If the card falls early you can make this bet before he's even finished dealing. Of course, if he takes it, he might win the game but he's sure to lose his money.

44 FIVE CARD TRICK

THE HOOK

Call it Three Card Monte, Find the Lady, Sidewalk Shuffle or a right rip-off, the urge to bet money on your ability to follow a card as it is shuffled around with a few others is irresistible. So much so that one famous gambler, Canada Bill Jones, once offered the Union Pacific Railroad $10,000 if they would let him work the old Three Card Monte on their trains. He promised that he would only defraud salesmen and Methodist preachers. Oddly enough, they didn't let him.

You have no compunction about playing this version of Monte on anyone who happens to come your way bearing a crisp ten spot. Instead of three cards you use five, which your punter will at first think is lessening his chances of winning. And that would be the case if it wasn't for the following offer:

"All I ask is that you follow the Queen. And to make it as simple as possible, I won't even shuffle them around. I'll just hold them, spread out like this. I'll show you the cards clearly so you can make sure you know where the Queen is. And then I'll turn them face-down. All you have to do is slide this paperclip onto the Queen. Snag the Queen and you're a winner. Snag anything else, and your money's mine."

You hold the cards spread out to show what you mean. The Queen is the middle card of the five. Doesn't look like there is anything funny going on. And as soon as the punter has taken out his tenner, you kindly hand him a paperclip in exchange. "Go on, just put it on the Queen" you say, adding quietly "make my day".

You don't use any sleight of hand. And as promised you don't shuffle any cards around. In fact he's certain that he's snagged the Queen. But when the cards are turned face-up, the punter is gobsmacked to find that he has made a grievous mistake – he accepted your bet.

THE CATCH

It's not the quickness of the hand deceiving the eye this time, but the eye is deceived all the same. The scam depends on a kind of optical illusion.

Take five playing cards, one of which is a Queen. Put the Queen in the middle and spread the five cards face-down as shown.

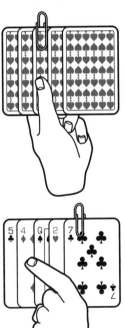

Put a paper clip on the card you think is the Queen i.e. the middle card.

Now turn the fan of cards over. You should be surprised to see that the clip is actually on the face card of the fan. You seem to have missed the Queen completely.

And that's what your punter discovers when he has a go – somehow he's totally missed his appointment with her Majesty. Pull the face card of the fan out and the paperclip with it and toss it to the table. Collect the tenner and pocket it while he grabs the cards to try it again for himself. It's rare that anyone gives the cards back – they're too busy trying their luck on the next sucker that passes by.

45 FAG BREAK

THE HOOK

Time to visit the pool table while your punters are complaining about your card cheating skills. But don't worry, you don't need to know blue chalk from blue cheese to make the following cool piece of showmanship work. It seems so impossible that people are not only happy to pay up, but they'll even pay you to show them how you cheated.

Walking up to a suitable punter (anyone in possession of a tenner) you say "Ever tried this? A guy showed it to me and I thought it was impossible." Borrow a cigarette – once again you've left yours in the machine – and stand it on its filter end in the centre of the table, unlit.

Then arrange three balls close around it, the cigarette standing right in the middle of them.

"Here's the challenge – you've got to hit the cue ball at those three balls, knocking them away but leaving the cigarette still standing."

Let your friend try. He'll find it is absolutely impossible to shoot the cue ball at the others without knocking over the cigarette. He can try all night if he wants to but he'll never do it.

Then say "I bet you a fiver I can do it." Now, he really wants to see this. He's been shooting balls all over the place and he just can't see how that cigarette can be left standing. He'll beg and whimper but you must be strong. Don't do this trick until his fiver is in your mit. It's just too good to give away for free.

THE CATCH

The laws of physics provide the solution for this little bit of hustling. When you arrange the balls for your friend to shoot at, you always make sure that the nearest ball is just touching the cigarette. And you always make sure that the two rear balls have a very slight gap between them. Doesn't matter how fast or slow he shoots, that cigarette will hit the deck.

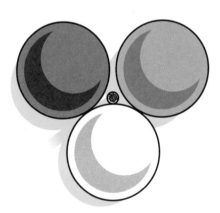

When you arrange the balls for your turn though you pack them tightly so each one is touching the other two but the cigarette is not touching any of them – that's absolutely essential.

Shoot at the ball nearest to you so that you hit it just off centre. Because the balls are packed tightly together they bounce off each other and cannot move inwards to disturb the cigarette. They fly apart leaving the cigarette still standing. It's an amazing thing to watch. So remarkable that your mate will be begging you for the secret of how you managed it. But secrets don't come cheap. It will cost him another fiver to learn – after all, it cost you fifty quid to learn... didn't it?

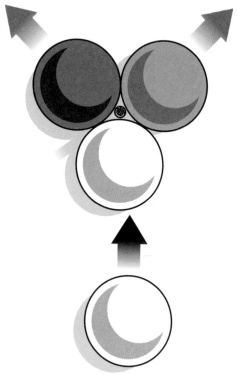

46 BLACK BALLED

THE HOOK

You're playing pool and, to be frank, you're not doing at all well. For once, the guy doing the hustling is not you. You'd taken him on thinking that he was a rank amateur but it turns out that he's a real pro. Finally his lucky streak runs out and it's your turn to shoot. The one thing you know is that if he gets a second chance you're stuffed. So you give the table a long cool look-over, as if studying all the angles, all the possibilities. You angle your cue this way and that, close one eye as you line up a shot, then move over to the other side of the table to spy out another.

Finally, you announce: "I think I've got you. If I'm right, you're not going to make another shot." He'll laugh in your face. And you in turn will laugh in his. You throw a tenner on the table with disdain. "Tenner says you won't make another shot." And now you look damned serious about it. And if he's half the player you think he is (hindsight's a wonderful thing) you know he's certain to take you up on your bet. He's got you beat, at least that's what he thinks, so why not take your tenner as well as his anticipated victory?

What he doesn't realise though is that although he may be a good player, you're a much better cheat.

THE CATCH

How can you beat a man that's already got you beat? You can't, so you'd better get used to the idea that you won't win this game. But you will win the bet.

And the reason is that you are going to commit a foul by deliberately sinking the black. And that means the game is over. As I said, you'll lose the game but win the bet, and that's where the money is.

Better be sure you can easily make the black before making the bet though. And be sure too that you're playing within rules that mean a foul of this kind means the end of the game and not just a couple of free shots to him.

And don't be too ashamed of taking his money because he'd certainly have been more than happy to take yours. Swindles work best when the sucker is absolutely certain that the odds are in his favour. And when a professional loses out to a rank amatuer, usually they'd much rather hand over the money quietly than make a scene about it.

BERMUDA TRIANGLE

THE HOOK

The Bermuda Triangle; a strange place where the punter's money mysteriously disappears, never to be seen again.

Taking the triangular frame used to line up the balls you balance it upright on the table and then stand a shot of whisky inside it. You challenge anyone to pick it up and turn it upside down without spilling the drink.

It sounds mad. Dangerous even. But mad and dangerous probably cover the bulk of your mates and you don't want some idiot swinging the frame around his head in a desperate attempt to meet the challenge. So you quickly add another condition. "Not only will I pick up the frame and turn it upside-down and not spill a drop of the liquid, but I'll do it half a dozen times in less than a minute."

And, just in case they thought there might be some cheating involved (as if), you tell them that you won't touch the glass or its contents. Anyone is welcome to make an attempt before you do but it'll cost them a tenner if they spill the whisky. And all breakages must be paid for. It'll also cost them a tenner if they want to see you do it.

THE CATCH

Centrifugal force is the answer, but it's not enough to pick up the rack and start swinging it round like a Russian hammer thrower. First you need to pick it up in the right way, and to do that you use the pool cue.

Stick the cue through the top of the frame until it sticks out the other side about a foot (thirty centimetres or gas mark five in old money).

Now comes the dangerous bit. Pick up the cue just less than half way along from the fat end with both hands and raise the frame off the table. Now, gently swing the assembly side to side on the cue. When you've picked up enough momentum, give the cue an extra swing and you'll be surprised to find that the frame will spin right round, upside-down and back again. And the liquid will stay firmly in the glass.

On a good day, with the wind in the right direction, you can keep the frame spinning and the whisky intact for a good half dozen revolutions. Be careful as you bring it to a halt though as, funnily enough, that's the trickiest part.

If you're feeling really brave, try it with a pint of beer.

48 HOT SPOT

THE HOOK

You've just taken the punter for an Ayrton and he's feeling justly peeved. What he needs is a little spiritual uplift, so you adopt your best evangelist tone and lay a double helping of happiness on it. "Look, I'm a generous guy. Yes indeed my friend, I'm feeling mighty generous of spirit tonight and feel that you of all people deserve a second chance."

Buy him a drink if it makes him feel better because a miserable man makes a poor punter. The joyful are more likely to put their capital at risk. Why, he's smiling already.

You put a ball on the spot and a coin on top of that. "Okay brother, here's the deal. Hit this ball with the cue ball and drop the coin right on the spot. Couldn't be simpler." Or so it seems. He's just got to win this bet, hasn't he? Alas, no.

THE CATCH

He'd stand a chance if he set the coin on top of the ball himself, but that's not a chance you're willing to give. When you place the coin on top of the ball, you don't place it dead centre. In fact it's deliberately placed at a slight angle. No matter how hard or slow the punter tries to hit the ball, the coin won't fall down and land on the table spot.

When you try it, you set the coin properly, square on top of the ball.

Give it a good hard smack with the cue ball and the coin will drop straight down to land right on top of the spot. Amen and hallelujah!

49 YOU'VE BEEN FRAMED

THE HOOK

Arrange three balls in a row, close to the side pocket. Place another ball (X) a short distance from them and challenge the punter to pocket all three balls with one shot without ever touching the X ball. Just as he's thinking about it, you lay down some conditions. No shots off the cushion, the cue ball can't leave the table and nothing must touch the X ball. Hmm...

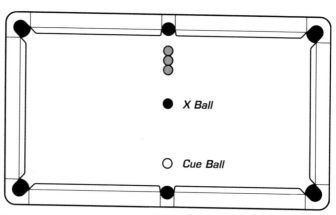

THE CATCH

The clue to this caper is in the title because you use the frame to accomplish this little piece of hocus pocus.

Set the frame around the X ball so that its top corner is almost touching the nearest of the three balls.

All you need to do to win the bet is hit the cue ball hard. It will strike the frame and, in turn, the corner of the frame will hit the other balls, knocking them right into the pocket.

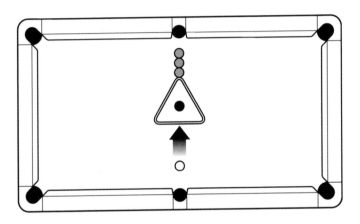

50 PRIVATE DICK

THE HOOK

Not everyone in the world will end up liking you, especially if you keep beating them at every game. Your scheming ways are building up a boil of resentment. Good, because in this scam you take advantage of the fact that your punter will risk any amount of money to see you fall on your backside.

It begins as a trick of the pick-a-card variety in which you offer to find the punter's secretly selected card. But something goes wrong; at least that's what the punter thinks. And he's so sure that you can't find his card that he's prepared to put money on it. But before he can say "abracadabra", once again you've made his money disappear.

THE CATCH

Don't worry if you've never done any magic before and you've got fingers like sausages. This card trick is really easy. It's the way you sell it that makes it an effective swindle.

Take a deck of cards, give it a shuffle and when you've finished, secretly note the bottom card. This is your 'key card'. Remember it.

Place the deck face down on the table and say "Let me show you a trick."

Ask the punter to cut the deck into two halves and then take the card he cut to, in other words the top card of the former lower half of the deck. That's his selected card. Tell him to remember it, and if he looks like he might be a bit of a plonker get him to show it to anyone else who is standing around. You can't be too careful. Many a good trick has been ruined by someone saying "I think it was the three. . . or was it the four, of those funny little clover things?"

When he has memorised it ask him to put it back, but instead of putting it back where he got it from you make him put it on top of the other half. Just say "Replace the card" and casually point to the top of the packet. This is critical to the success of the trick, so don't get it wrong otherwise you're going to end up as the plonker.

Ask him to pick up the other (bottom) half of the deck and drop it on top of the other. In effect, what you've done is secretly place your key card above his selected card. Tell him to cut the deck again and complete the cut. He can do this several times. In fact, no matter how many times he does it, your key card will always stay right next to his selected one. By the end of the cutting the punter should be convinced that his card is lost in the deck, and if he doesn't know where it is, how could you?

Looks like a pretty good trick so far. Pick up the deck, saying "What a lot of people don't realise is that when they take a card they leave fingerprints on it. It's true. I can find your card just by examining your fingerprints."

Ask the punter to hold out his thumb. Take a good look at it in a Sherlock Holmes stylee, then nod knowingly and murmur "shouldn't be too difficult."

Look carefully at the back of the top card of the deck, then, apparently satisfied that this isn't the card you are looking for, turn it over and deal it face up onto the table. The punter will think you are looking for fingerprints. You're not. You're looking for your key-card because the next card after it will be his.

Keep turning over cards and dealing them into a pile on the table. Make the pile a messy one so that all the cards can be seen at once.

Every now and then you take another look at the punter's thumb, then compare it to the back of the top card. At some point during your Sherlock charade your key card will show up. Don't bat an eyelid when it does. Deal it onto the table just like the others. The next card in the pack will be the punter's card. Remember it and deal it onto the table too, but don't stop; continue examining the backs of the following cards, turning them over and putting them on the table.

Your punter will be confused by this. He knows you've gone right past his selected card. And if you keep talking up your detective skills "I've never been wrong..." he'll start to feel a bit smug.

Let a half-dozen or so cards go by and then look at the back of the next card with satisfaction as though you've found something. Then look at his thumb. Then back at the card. "The next card I turn over will be yours," you say. The punter will assume you mean the card on top of the deck and since he can see his card already on the table, he won't believe you. Reel him in, saying "Do you think that's possible?" Whatever he says, turn his response into a wager. "Ten quid says it is. Ten pounds says the next card I turn over will be yours."

He will be absolutely sure you've got it wrong and his tenner shouldn't be long in making an entrance. Put yours on the table beside it. Then say "Okay, ten pounds that the next card I turn over will be yours." Pause, so the full consequence of what you have said sinks in. Then reach over to the pile of cards on the table, pull out his card and turn it face down!

Elementary my dear Watson.

51 CASE DISMISSED

THE HOOK

As far as the unlucky punter is concerned, the one redeeming feature of being taken by the *Private Dick* trick is that he might be able to use it on someone else. He's therefore grateful that you've taught him exactly how to do it.

He's thankful too that you've made him practice the trick on you. You wouldn't want him going out trying it on some poor mug without getting the details just right, would you?

Okay, all he needs to do now is find himself a punter. But look; who's this walking into the pub? It's one of your dodgy mates. "He's a bit of an idiot" you say. "Shouldn't have much difficulty with him." Chance to get your money back. Maybe even a bit more. Off you go mate, get it while you can."

And as he ambles away to hook his first victim, you get the drinks in because, once again, you won't be paying for them.

THE CATCH

The punter has, of course, been set up. While he thinks he's onto a winner, the reality is that he's about to double what he lost before. The scam goes like this:

He follows all your instructions and reaches the stage where he knows the identity of your mate's card. He can see it right there on the table. The trouble is, your mate knows this trick too. And he knows you've sent this poor sod over to have his wallet ransacked. So when the would-be Sherlock says "I bet you ten quid that the next card I turn over will be yours," your mate answers "Nah, that's impossible!"

Sherlock will tell him that ten quid says it's not. To which your mate says "Ten quid? It's worth twenty! Twenty quid says that the next card you turn over won't be mine."

Talk about pennies from heaven. Sherlock is secretly congratulating himself on making more money from this trick than you did.

"Are we on?" asks your mate. He extends a hand to Sherlock. And as Sherlock is shaking it, he uses his other hand to turn over the cards on the table and mix them around. With them all now face down, Sherlock has just lost his first case.

52 CUT THROAT

THE HOOK

"This is a gentleman's game," you say as you shuffle a deck of cards. "You cut, I cut, and whoever gets the highest card wins."

You ask him to start by cutting off some cards. He does, and cuts to an eight. Now it's your turn. You cut deep, look at the card, and say "Nine, I win!" and then replace the cards on the deck.

Which would be great if you really did cut a nine spot but your punter is none too sure. You didn't actually show him the card you cut to.

"Didn't I explain? This is a gentleman's game. We both trust each other. Don't we?" Truth is he doesn't trust you one bit and he watches carefully as you shuffle the deck again and place it on the table.

"Once more" you say, indicating that the punter should cut the cards again. This time he cuts a Jack. You make your cut and declare a Queen, but again you quickly replace your cards before he gets a chance to see what you actually did cut to.

"Don't you believe me? Look!" You pick up the deck and spread through it, finding a Queen. "That's the one." Then smile inanely.

"Let's try again. This time, I'll cut first." You do and declare a King. Not surprisingly when the punter makes his cut he's finally caught onto the game. "I've got an ace" he says, replacing the cards. He beat you, or so it seems. In fact, as the punter will soon find out, you've just beat him.

THE CATCH

As soon as the punter claims he cut to an ace, you bet him that he didn't. And he'll probably take it too, expecting that he can do exactly what you did and just pick up the deck, spread through the cards and say, "That's the ace I cut to."

Except, as you might have already guessed, he can't. There are no aces in that deck. You put them in your pocket before you began. Fancy, him trying to cheat you of all people!

53 COLOUR BLIND

THE HOOK

"Name a colour – red or black?" you say to the punter. He chooses red and you offer to play him a game of *Colour Blind*. He's never heard of it so, always ready to share your knowledge, you offer to teach him.

"It's simple. You shuffle the deck and then put it down on the table. Then you turn cards over two at a time. If they are both red, you get them. If they are both black, I get them. If one is red and the other is black, nobody gets them. Clear?"

Crystal, and so is the bet: "Whoever ends up with the most cards wins the game. To make sure it's fair, you get to shuffle the cards." The punter shuffles. He deals. You win.

THE CATCH

I'm not sure exactly how this bet works, only that it does, provided you are using a full deck of fifty-two cards. Before you start playing you sneak two red cards out of the deck. If the cards are dealt as described, there will always be more black pairs than red pairs.

It's only when the punter chooses the colour that you tell him exactly what the bet is. If he chooses red, say "Whoever has the most cards wins." If he chooses black, say "Whoever has the least cards wins." Either way it will be you.

54 CHASE THE ACE

THE HOOK

You show three cards: an ace, two and three of clubs, and hand them to the punter as you invite him to play *Chase the Ace*. "It's the same as Find the Lady," you say, "except you get to mix the cards and I do the betting."

He shuffles the three cards up so that no-one knows which is which. Then you ask him to deal one card to himself, one to you and the last card to him. He's got two and you've got one.

"Pick up your two cards, look at them. You might have the ace, or you might not. Either way I want you to deal any card except the ace face up onto the table."

He does, leaving you with one face down card each. "Now, you already have the advantage over me. You've seen two of the cards so you already know whether I've got the ace or whether you have. But I've seen nothing. Is that right?"

He'll agree that it is. "And yet a quid says I can find the ace. And to prove it, I'll give you ten chances to win."

Sounds fair and yet Lady Luck has already sided with you; it won't be long before his pockets are as empty as a politician's promise.

THE CATCH

You won't win this bet every time. But you will win in the long run which is why you play for low stakes over ten rounds.

What the punter doesn't realise is that by dealing himself two of the three cards he's also giving himself two chances out of three of having the ace.

It doesn't matter that he knows where the ace is or that he has turned one of his cards face up. You always bet that the ace is in the hand that originally held two cards. And two out of three times you will be right. Over a long sequence of betting, you will win.

To vary the game have him sometimes deal the two cards to you. Makes no difference; you always bet on the card left over from the hand that once held two cards.

And to confuse him further, every now and then you take three different cards out of the pack and nominate one of them as the card you'll follow.

If you feel that the mathematics of the game really are passing the punter by, then use four cards and have him deal three into one hand and then turn two of them over. If he'll fall for that, he'll fall for anything.

 LIMBO

THE HOOK

Let's face it; you're a lousy pool player. You couldn't pot a ball if there were a dozen pockets on the table. That's why if you want to beat the sharks you're going to have to do it with brains rather than skill. And if you want to try some of the following bets you'd better be fast on your feet as well. Or at least have some big mates standing by.

You pick up a cue, study it carefully and pretend to weigh it between your hands. Then you lay it across the table, with each end resting on opposite cushions near the side pockets.

With the cue in that position you challenge the punter to pick up a ball and roll it under the cue.

It doesn't look impossible. The punter will think that if he rolls the ball hard enough at the thin end of the cue it might be enough to make it jump up out of the way. It won't. And in any case you tell him "When the ball's gone under, the cue has to be in the same position that it started." That should give him pause for thought.

THE CATCH

All you asked him to do was roll the ball under the cue. And that's exactly what you do as you roll the ball along the floor... under the table!

You can get caught out on this – always check the table you're working with to make sure that there is a gap below it to roll the ball through; some automated tables don't have one.

 **HEAD SOUTH**

THE HOOK

"An eight year old kid could do this one... with twenty years practice" you say. "All you have to do is reverse the triangle like this".

There are ten balls in the frame and they make a neat triangle which points north. You then turn the frame around, complete with balls, until the tip points south.

"That's all you have to do; turn the triangle around so that the balls point in the opposite direction. There are two problems though. The first is that you can't use the frame. The second is that you can only move three of the balls. Move three balls and make the triangle point the opposite way. You've got five minutes. Off you go!"

THE CATCH

This is a real brain-strainer. It's so easy when you use the triangle but doing the same thing by moving only three of the balls is an entirely different kettle of worms. It can be done and, as usual, the answer is simple when you know how. Fortunately for you, the punter doesn't.

The illustration explains everything you need to know. The balls at the tips of the triangle are the ones that you need to move. The only thing the punter will be moving is money from his wallet to yours.

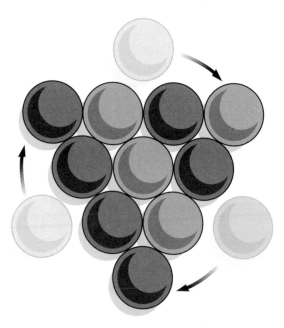

🂢 THE MONEY SHOT

THE HOOK

There you are playing the pub legend Typhoon Ted, house champion for more years than you care to remember. Ted is as daft as the brush he's usually to be found pushing along the high street, but he's a damn good pool player and, as usual, you take a beating at the table. Still, all is not lost and at the end of the game you bluster Typhoon into a little wager.

First you get a tenner off him, square it up with one of your own and fasten them together with a paperclip you just happen to have handy. The clipped notes are placed on the table and then a ball set on top of them both. You place the black just in front of a side pocket and the cue ball on the opposite side of the table.

"The challenge is to start with a ball on top of the notes. Then you have to pot the black in the side pocket without hitting that ball. What's more, you can't hit a cushion and the cue ball mustn't leave the table. Winner takes all."

Even Typhoon Ted will think this is impossible unless he's a wizard at

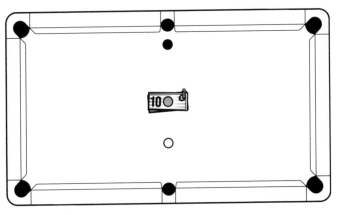

making curve shots. But his cash is already on the table and he won't be getting it back unless he figures out how to make that shot.

THE CATCH

When Typhoon Ted has tried and failed, you repeat the conditions of the challenge. "The ball starts on top of the notes." As you say this you pick the tenners up and roll them into a tube. Use the paperclip to keep the tube closed. Then balance the ball on top of the rolled up notes.

"You can't hit that ball but I didn't say anything about hitting the notes"

You now shoot the cue ball at the rolled up notes. It knocks the tube out of the way and, if you've hit it true, carries on and pots the black.

"No cushions or jump shots either. I think you'll agree that fulfils the terms of the bet." Best buy Typhoon a drink after this one. Looks like he's had the wind knocked right out of him.

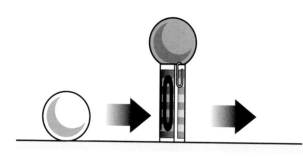

58 CUELESS

THE HOOK

You've done just about everything but actually play a game of pool to achieve your near legendary reputation. Once again you're about to display your prowess when it comes to ball control. And this time you're not even going to use a cue; just one finger will do the trick!

You place a ball up on the cushion at one end of the table with your forefinger holding it in place. Your punter does the same with another ball. The challenge is to press down on the ball and squirt it up the table as far as you can. Your bet is that you can squirt your ball further than they can.

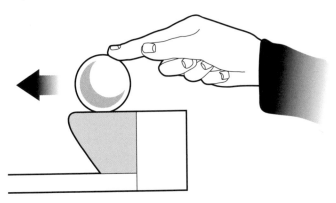

Now the great thing about this challenge is that everyone can play along – so long as they have a tenner that is. And the more the merrier, for you will indeed beat all comers. But let them all take their turn first and mark their distances on the table with chalk. Then, show them how an expert does it.

THE CATCH

This simple challenge is trickier than it looks. Anyone pushing down hard on the ball in the hope that mere pressure will cause it to travel further up the table will be in for a shock. Pressing down causes backspin and so the ball not only won't squirt very far but after a short while will start rolling backwards.

Not so when you press down on your ball however because you've secretly wet the tip of your finger, either with saliva, or just dip it in your drink when no-one is looking. This lessens the friction between the ball and your fingertip and so prevents backspin; you'll have no trouble getting the ball all the way up the table. From then on, it's but a short step to a night of free drinks.

59 BOX CLEVER

THE HOOK

You play a little game of monte with the punter. He hides a ten pound note in one of three packets of cigarettes while your back is turned. The bet is this: if you find the box containing the tenner, you keep it. If you fail, you pay him double the stake. Looks like a winner for him but the truth is you cannot fail.

THE CATCH

You need three packets of cigarettes for this trick. At first glance they all look alike, but in fact one of them is marked so that you can distinguish it from the other two. It can be any kind of a secret mark; a nick in the box, a pencil dot, a slightly dented corner. Anything that you will notice but the punter won't.

Now pay attention – there's money resting on this. Set the three cigarette boxes out in front of the punter with the marked one to your left.

You can see the mark from where you are.

Tell him that when your back is turned he should place his tenner inside one of the boxes then put it back in position.

Okay, let's assume he's done that. Now tell him to swap the positions of the other two boxes. And when he's satisfied, he should just make sure that all the boxes are once again in a straight line.

Believe it or not, as soon as you turn around you will be able to tell him which box contains the money. It's easy. Just look for the box you marked. If the box is still at the left end of the row, then that's the box with the money.

If the marked box is at the right end of the row, then the money is in the middle box. And if the marked box is in the middle of the row, then the money is in the box on the right.

Nothing more to it. You will win his money every time. And with a little bit of practice you'll be able to calculate which box the money is in no matter where the marked box starts. It's just a matter of applying a little logic and commonsense. It also makes an ideal follow up to *Matchbox Monte*. Take the matches out and use the punter's money instead.

A word of warning though. Never turn your back on a punter unless you have a friend nearby to keep an eye on him. You don't want them mixing the boxes up any old how the moment your eyes are off him. That wouldn't be fair play, would it?

60 DICING WITH DEBT

THE HOOK

Dice are the ultimate symbols of fate. The very tools of Lady Luck herself, used since time immoral in games of chance the world over. If you could control the dice, you could control the future. Okay, maybe that's a little overstated, but you could certainly win a few quid from your gullible mates. So, after a skilful game like backgammon, in which you exhibited no skill whatsoever, you redeem yourself with this little stunt.

"What do you think the chances are of us rolling the same numbers on the dice?" you ask. The punter tries his best to calculate the odds but frankly he hasn't a clue how to so he'll probably come up with some nonsense like "million to one." Fine. You're not running a course on probability. As long as he realises it's difficult, that's all that matters.

"Well, I bet that if you throw these two dice, I might not be able to throw the exact same numbers as you – that would be nigh on impossible – but I bet I can throw the same total. So if you throw ten, I'll throw ten."

Let this sink in. It's actually highly unlikely that you'd be able to do this but it lays the foundation for the next line you're going to bait him with.

"I'm so confident that I reckon I can let you throw the dice, add up the top numbers and the bottom numbers and then I'll take the same two dice and throw exactly the same total. How does that sound?"

It sounds very impressive. Surely, it's twice as difficult as your first proposition? You'll match whatever total he throws. And that includes not just the top numbers but the bottom ones as well. What are the odds on that?

THE CATCH

The odds are 100% in your favour!

All good dice, and this includes ones found in kid's board games as well as casinos, are made in a particular way. The top and bottom numbers of every die (yes, that *is* the singular!) always add up to seven. Not a lot of people know that, not even Michael Caine. And if your punter happens to be one of the people who do then he won't accept the bet in the first place and all you've cost yourself is mild embarrassment.

This design factor means that if the punter rolls two dice and adds both top and bottom numbers, he will always arrive at a total of fourteen. And if you roll two dice, although you will probably not end up with the same numbers showing on top, they will also total fourteen. It's a dead cert.

You disguise this oddity of the dice by first having him roll the two dice and add up the top numbers. Then have him turn one dice over and add the bottom number. Then he turns the second dice over and adds the bottom number on that one. That way he reaches the total of fourteen without ever noticing that each dice added up to seven. Go through the same procedure when totalling the numbers on your dice.

Oh, and don't try it twice on the same punter. That really would be pushing your luck.

FOUR
MASTERMIND

"BEHIND EVERY GREAT FORTUNE
THERE IS A GREAT CRIME."
- HONORE DE BALZAC

 WEAKEST LINK

THE HOOK

Whatever happened to the good old British pub? That comfy place that was just like home – dirty and full of nutters. A place where you could get a quiet pint, a game of darts and be sure to hear some old bloke banging on about whippets.

Okay it was boring, but at least there weren't any pub quizzes. When you got caught under-age drinking by your history teacher he didn't ask you to name five dead American Presidents for ten points.

Trouble is there's a new breed of 'experts' who, instead of spending their time working on genetic engineering at Oxford, are sitting at the Fool and Bladder shouting "Easy!". Time for revenge.

Within earshot of your local 'expert', your mate, who you've primed in advance, holds up a bit of paper and says, "No way, not in sixty seconds you can't."

"Maybe I can't, but I bet Keith can. He's been pub quiz champ two years running, haven't you Keith?" you say.

"Three." corrects Keith, and with praise as bait, wanders over to the killing field.

"Keith could do it easily, couldn't you Keith, answer one poxy quiz question in sixty seconds?"

Now Keith is not going to wager any money on this stunt - not right away anyhow. So you wring the cash out of him by appealing to his ego. "I'll bet a tenner he can. You can do it can't you Keith?"

He'll hum and haw but the main thing he'll want to know is where the question came from. "My kid's school" is always a good answer. "That Millionaire quiz" is another. But "The pub quiz down the road" is sure to hook him.

So put your tenner on the table then look at Keith and ask him for his.

I mean, if you've got such confidence in him, shouldn't he have confidence in himself? You might need a crowbar to get his wallet open but the one thing more precious to a trivia addict than his cash is his pride.

THE CATCH

Take the question paper off your stooge and place it face down in front of Keith. Have someone time him, turn the paper over and off you go. Here's the question:

Marie's father has five daughters:

1 - Chacha

2 - Cheche

3 - Chichi

4 - Chocho

5 - ? ? ? ? ? ?

What is the fifth daughter's name?

Keith, if he's bright, will stare at it for maybe thirty seconds, work out the vowel sequence and come up with the name of "Chuchu" – easy. But he's wrong. The name of the fifth daughter is "Marie". Didn't his teacher tell him to read the question carefully?

One thing's for sure. He won't forget your name in a hurry. Be nice though – at least give him the dignity of waiting until he's gone before you and your mate buy the next round using his cash.

62 CASH IN HAND

THE HOOK

You hold up your closed fist; an unmistakable challenge to Einstein, Keith's best and equally brainy mate, and say "I've got three coins in my hand, and they add up to eight pence."

"So?" says Einstein.

"So, one of them isn't a five-pence piece," you reply. He's been playing that quiz machine all evening like a man possessed and making a killing so it's time you relieved him of some of his loose change. He thinks about it for a while. Eight pence, three coins and yet one of them isn't a five-pence piece. You can see his forehead furrowing. Finally he decides that such a thing can't be right.

"Oh yes it can," you say, "And I'll bet a tenner that I'm telling the truth: three coins, they add up to eight pence and yet one of them isn't a five pee."

"You're bluffing."

"Am I?"

When you see the sweat starting to collect in those furrows you know you've got him.

"Let's see your tenner" you say, taking a note from your pocket. It's unfair really. He's an information junkie. He wants to know. He must know, even if he has to pay ten quid for the answer. You rustle the crisp tenner between your fingers. He still thinks you're bluffing, but he doesn't know for sure. The only thing for certain is that it's going to cost him to find out. Soon he will be stacking the stream of gold that tumbled from the quiz machine. And a tenner of it will be yours.

THE CATCH

When you find a man of words it's nice to beat him up with them so be careful how you phrase this bet. When you open your hand you reveal a five-pence, a two-pence and a one-pence. That's eight-pence in total. Ah, you think, but when Einstein sees the coins he is going to say, "You said one of the coins wasn't a five-pence piece." So you did, and to prove it you pick up the one-pence piece saying, "This one isn't a five-pence piece," and then the two-pence piece "and, now that I come to think of it, actually this one isn't either." Game, set and match.

 WORD UP

THE HOOK

Einstein is at the bar sipping his grapefruit juice and his girl Marilyn is by his side with the cheapest drink that money can buy. He's a clever guy but mean as hell. *Who Wants To Be A Millionaire* is on the television and he's shouting out the answers. Marilyn's not impressed. She's seen it all before. He's just such a smartarse. But there's smart and then there's street smart.

Sensing your moment, you go up to him and say "Tell me Einstein, how long do you think it would take to think up a hundred words that didn't have the letter A in them?" Knowing him it won't be long. So you up the stakes. "Okay, how long to think of a hundred different words that don't have the letters A or B in them?" Again, that's no problem for Einstein but wouldn't it be better if Marilyn could name them? I mean, Einstein doesn't even think she knows a hundred words. Which is great, because here's the bet:

"I bet that me and Marilyn can name a hundred words without the letters A, B, C, J, K, M, P, Q or Z in them. Can't we Marilyn? And we'll do it in less than five minutes."

Marilyn will now have the look of a rabbit caught in headlights. "No way, I can't do that" she protests. But you don't listen to her. "In fact, I'll just name five of the words and I bet Marilyn can name the other ninety-five, isn't that right Marilyn?"

Now that's just too good an offer to turn down. Whatever other charms Marilyn may possess, she isn't known for her intellect, and before you can say "'phone a friend" the bait has been taken and the money is as good as yours.

THE CATCH

When called upon to deliver you start to count: "One, two, three, four, five" and then you turn to Marilyn and prompt her to continue the count up to one-hundred, saying "You can continue from there Marilyn, one hundred words and believe it or not, none of them have the letters A, B, C, J, K, M, P, Q or Z in them. By the way, what are you drinking? He's paying."

64 OUT FOR THE COUNT

THE HOOK

You walk into the bar and see Einstein, alone this time, watching *The Weakest Link* on television. Once again he's getting all the answers right and everyone around the bar is completely cheesed off. You get the drinks in, go up to Einstein, pat him on the back and say "Nice going. You never seem to get anything wrong, do you mate? In fact, I don't think you could get a question wrong if you tried." He'll quite rightly look at you with some suspicion, remembering the last bet you won. So you reassure him that you have no hidden agenda, which of course you do. "No, really, I bet if I asked you some questions, you couldn't give me five wrong answers in a row."

Wrong answers? He's never given a wrong answer in his life so it's best to clarify what you mean. "I mean, I ask you five questions and you give me five deliberately wrong answers. For instance, I ask you your name, you tell me it's Yoda. I ask you what two plus two is, you say five. Got it?"

He's got it but you've still got to reel him in. "In fact you're so bleedin' brainy that I'm prepared to bet ten quid that you can't give me five wrong answers." You lay your dosh on the table. He thinks about it. "Go on Einstein," you say, like a man trying to do him a good turn. A man trying to make amends for taking his money along with his dignity. "I know you'll win this one." His tenner hits the table, Queen Elizabeth blinking in the light, and you proceed to hit him with the questions. Need I say he doesn't get them all wrong?

THE CATCH

Pull this one off and you'll get an Oscar. Here are the questions:

Point to his tenner on the table and ask: "What's that?" He can answer with anything he likes as long as he doesn't give the right answer. "Good, that was an easy one." Turn to Marilyn and say, "What's her name?" Hmm. He'll be looking for a bit of trickery there. There isn't any and after due thought he'll give a nonsense answer, probably something Freudian like "Mother".

"Point to one of the drinks and ask, "Is this glass full or empty?" He gives an answer. Pause for thought and then ask, in a very casual way, "How many questions is that?" Say it as if you've lost count. Now he may smell a rat at this point and if he does, it's you, because this is a trick question. It is possible he'll give you the right answer, three, in which case he loses the bet. But a smart guy like Einstein will probably see through it, and he'll give you some other answer. This is where your acting skills come in.

"You clever sod!" Give a laugh and pretend to have been caught at your own game. Einstein has beaten you. Let him think he's won. "You did well, mate, you deserve a drink for that. Marilyn, get him a drink, the boy done good." And then very casually ask "Have you heard that one before?" And lulled by your manner he will say "No." And that's when he loses the bet, because you said you'd ask him five questions, and this is the fifth. He'll need that drink.

65 WHAT'S THE SCORE?

THE HOOK

Today's the day of the F.A. Cup Final and Fred the Football Freak is by the bar recalling the outcome of the last fifty finals and speculating about this one. There's nothing he doesn't know when it comes to soccer statistics and the guys are asking questions because they're running a sweepstake on who is going to score the first goal. So you wander up and say "I've got a bet for you. Never mind who scores first, I bet I can tell you what the score will be before the match even starts." He'll reel out some figures and probabilities and talk about whose playing and in what positions, but before he can bore you to tears you interrupt "No, what I mean Fred, is that right here and now I can tell you what the score will be before they've even touched the ball. In fact, I've written it down."

You take an envelope out of your pocket and place it on the bar. "And I bet you a tenner I'm right. Anyone else want to take that bet?" Look around for any likely punters as you take out your wallet and lay a tenner on the envelope to show that you mean business. Unless you've already cleaned out this neighbourhood, you're about to go home a winner.

THE CATCH

You said you knew what the score would be before the match started. So you did. It was nil-nil. It always is before the match starts, and that's what you wrote down in the envelope! Make sure the exit's in sight and you're wearing your trainers when you work this one.

66 PROPHETEERING

THE HOOK

Keith's back. He's still not forgiven you for that five daughters question and Einstein has been telling him what a complete conman you are. So has Marilyn. Well, you didn't think it would last did you? Basically, he's looking for revenge. And to make matters worse it's raining outside and your pockets are as empty as Marilyn's head. So you quickly conjure up another bet.

"Keith, what do you know about wildlife?" you ask. Fact is he knows more than David Attenborough but don't let that stop you. "Well, here's a question for you. It was the rain that inspired me" you say, lying. "And there's a tenner for a correct answer. Ready?" Taking his blank look as a 'yes', you've got yourself a bet. "Okay, tenner to you if you get it, tenner to me if you lose." Without pausing to give him chance to back out, you say "Well, it's a biblical question: how many animals did Moses take on the ark with him?"

A bright guy like Keith will usually answer almost immediately. "Two of each." And, of course, he'd be wrong.

THE CATCH

The correct answer is none. Moses didn't take any animals onto the ark. That was Noah!

Of course it's just possible that Keith catches you out on this one. He might be sharper than you imagine. Somewhat cockily he could say "It wasn't Moses, it was Noah." In which case you play the fool, saying "Oh, yeah. Stupid me. I could have sworn it was Moses. We'll forget that one. Who was Moses anyway?" Immediately you'll get a long and dull discourse on Moses and, with his irresistible urge to show off his knowledge, Keith will have forgotten entirely about the bet so you won't have to pay out. There will always be another chance to drain the brain of his cash.

67 TIME OF THE MONTH

THE HOOK

Looking along the bar you see that Keith has got himself a PDA. Either that or he's trying to beam himself up to another planet. For the uninitiated, a PDA is a personal digital assistant. It's an electronic miracle, a hand-held computer in which you can keep notes, your diary or, as Keith is doing now, quiz questions. Does everything a notepad and pen does except costs a lot more and if you drop it on the floor your entire life disappears. Still, it provides you with a good opening salvo in the perpetual war of wagers.

"I've heard they're really bad for you those things."

"What are you on about?" says Keith, tapping his tiny screen.

"Read it in the paper. They say people depend on them too much. They forget the everyday things of life."

"Like what?" He switches the machine off and puts it away, suddenly looking a little scared that you've set your beady eyes on it and might be about to embark on some devious scheme in an attempt to make it your own. As if.

"For instance," you say "before computers were invented, you exercised your brain more. If you wanted to remember something you used a poem or a little rhyme or saying. That way it stuck in your mind. I bet your memory's not half as good since you got that thing."

As usual Keith will disagree and so, for the obligatory tenner, you offer to put him to the test. "Okay, remember the old poem about the number of days in a month? Well, without looking at the diary in your computer, how many months have thirty days in them?"

He'll smile. PDAs aren't like mobile phones. They don't toast your brain. The old rhyme is as clear to him now as it was when he first heard it. Which is great, because as long as he starts working out whether each month has thirty or thirty-one days, you've trapped him in yet another mind field.

THE CATCH

Talking about computers and the old rhyme has led Keith down a blind alley. There's only one answer to the problem and it is unlikely to occur to him. Every month has thirty days in it, except for February!

Think about it. And if it still makes no sense, maybe you should get yourself one of those PDAs.

68 SHAKEN AND STIRRED

THE HOOK

To the mastermind, nothing is more attractive than a puzzle to be solved. Not even the lovely Marilyn. When the likes of Einstein and Keith get together over a puzzle, the rest of the world might as well not exist.

You offer to show them something you saw on television last night. "Absolutely amazing, no one could get it," you say, implying that if either of the brainboxes were able to solve it, they would be worthy of your praise, and the tenner you're offering. Should they not manage to get it, then they owe you a tenner. "They only had a minute to do it on TV," you explain "but I'll give you five minutes to make it fair. After all, some of the kids on that quiz show are pretty clever." That should wind them up.

The puzzle looks simple as you lay out eight matches to make a simple diagram of two glasses. "Imagine they're two Martini glasses. All we need now is an olive." You take out a coin and invite one of the punters to place the olive into one of the glasses.

"Here's the puzzle. You can't touch the olive but you've got to get it out of the glass. You can touch the matches though. The only problem is that you can only move two of them. That's it; move two matches and get the olive out of the glass. Your five minutes start now!"

And it will be five very slow minutes indeed for the two unfortunate punters.

THE CATCH

This puzzle has been around for a long time and it's usually done with just one 'glass'. But using two glasses makes it even stronger, especially if your punters really are puzzle addicts. The second glass acts as a red herring, making them think of building an extra glass in the space between the existing ones. And it prevents them discovering the real solution, which is to simply rearrange the matches so that one glass is now upside-down.

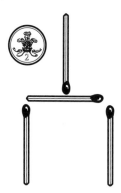

It doesn't matter which glass the punters drop the coin in to start with. Just make sure that the two glasses are more than a matchstick's length apart. You want it to look as if their proximity offers a solution. But you don't want any clever dick actually finding one!

⑥⑨ DIAMONDS ARE FOREVER

THE HOOK

Another match puzzle and one that seems to offer some hope of a solution to the brainy ones. In reality it's just another scam.

You start by laying out 5 matches in a diamond formation.

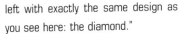

"The bet is to take away three matches and then add two. And yet be left with exactly the same design as you see here: the diamond."

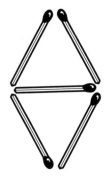

With challenges of this kind it's always best to set a time limit and for very good reasons. Firstly, some people will take all day about it and for the sake of pride just refuse to give up even when you've got them beat. And secondly, you want your money! Five minutes is usually a good enough allowance but even if you gave them the entire day they probably wouldn't solve this little stunner.

THE CATCH

Expect to be questioned all the way through this one as the punter tries to solve the puzzle. But be firm and only repeat the terms of the wager, that they should take away three matches and add two and still be left with exactly the same diamond design as they started with.

Here's how you do it. First press your fingers against the lower triangle of matches and then draw them down towards you, saying "I've taken away three matches."

Now pick up the upper two matches and add them to the triangle, once again making up the diamond shape as you say, "And I add two matches.

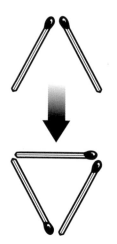

I've taken away three and added two. And the diamond looks exactly the way it did before."

They may kick themselves but they can't complain you didn't do exactly as you promised. Now it's their turn to do exactly as they promised, and hand over their hard-earned.

10 PYRAMID POWER

THE HOOK

Another brain buster to test even the most geometrically adept. You lay three matches on the table, saying "It's easy to make a triangle out of three matches but how many triangles can you make out of six?"

There will be some discussion about this, to which you will listen carefully as if weighing up the answers. Then, having heard what your potential punters have to say you make the following wager: "I bet I can make more triangles than you can. Not the same amount, but more." Let that sink in for a while. They've already explored some of the options and they can't see how you can possibly do better than they can unless, of course, you cheat. You quickly reassure them on that point.

"I'll make more triangles than you can. And the conditions are that you can't break any matches, you can't add any more matches and that all the triangles must be the same size. Tenner says I can. And remember, I have to beat you to win. Time limit on the contest is five minutes. And I'll take on everyone at the same time. Is that a deal?"

Assuming that their combined heads can beat your one, they accept the challenge. And unless they know something you don't, the most they will be able to make with their matches is two triangles. I've never seen anyone make three. You, however, are about to make four!

THE CATCH

The secret to this stunt is given away in the title. Your four triangles are made up of the sides of a three-dimensional pyramid.

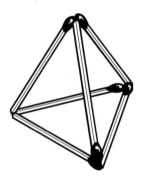

When constructing it, work on a tablecloth rather than a polished bar top. It will take a bit of care to build but it can be done quickly once you've got the knack.

The pyramid might not be as impressive as the ancient Egyptian ones but it does possess a curse - everyone who sees it will lose money!

11 THEORY OF RELATIVITY

THE HOOK

This is one for the puzzle brigade. You know the kind. They say things like "A plane crashes on the border between Mexico and America. And it's full of Swedish pastry chefs. Where do they bury the survivors?" And if you're a couple of sheets to the wind you spend the next half hour talking about international law. At the end of which the smartarse who asked the question laughs and says "Idiot. You don't bury survivors." Ha ha.

Well, this one's for him. Get him talking about his favourite topic: himself and his seemingly endless knowledge of trivia. Then hit him with this one. "Can a man legally marry his widow's sister?" It has all the hallmarks of a trick question and he'll seize the bait immediately, explaining that if the man has a widow then he must be dead. And dead men can't marry.

"That's not true," you say. "I think a man can marry his widow's sister. In fact I'm sure of it." So sure that you're willing to place a small wager on it.

THE CATCH

It is in fact possible. The loophole through which dead men can marry their widow's sister is simple. They marry the sister first!

So a man met two sisters, married one of them and then, realising what a nutter she was, got divorced. He then married the other sister. Unfortunately she was even madder than the first and drove him to an early grave. His death wasn't in vain though as it enabled you to say that a dead man did indeed legally marry his widow's sister, thereby inadvertently making you a tenner!

72 THE PRICE IS RIGHT

THE HOOK

You can turn almost any trick question into a bet if you set it up in the right way. It's a matter of conjuring up a believable story and making it a challenge that's impossible to resist. So when you say to your mate Mickey "No, no don't tell them, let's see if they can guess", Keith and Einstein's ears start to burn.

"Guess what?" says Keith.

"Guess how much Mickey's latest purchase just cost him." you reply. "I'll give you a clue. One costs a pound but you can get twelve for two quid. And Mickey's bought a hundred and forty four. How much do you reckon it cost him?"

Mickey nods. He would; he's been promised half the winnings. "And if you can tell me what Mickey paid, I'll give you a tenner. But if you can't – and I'll give you a minute to discuss it – you owe me a tenner."

And since no one, especially Keith and Einstein, like an unsolved mystery, the bet is almost sure to be on.

THE CATCH

The answer is three quid! Sounds improbable until you prompt Mickey to pull the merchandise out of his pocket. Keith and Einstein should be feeling pretty stupid as Mickey produces three plastic numbers for his front door. That's right; a pound each and he just happens to live at a hundred and forty four!

73 DIVIDE AND CONQUER

THE HOOK

Okay, so you knew it was going to happen. Keith and Einstein have taken the pub quiz trophy again and won themselves twenty quid and a warm bottle of sparkling wine. So what?

So what? They've got twenty unexpected quid on them, that's what. And you've got just enough time to get to them before they reach the bar and squander it all on pork scratchings.

"You did well there boys," you say, preparing for the kill. "There's not much you two don't know about is there?" With any luck your goading will encourage a bit of bragging on their part. You follow it up, saying "But I've got a little problem that might just baffle even you."

People who have just won money often have a carefree attitude to their winnings. That's why most gamblers usually end up broke. And that's why Keith and Einstein will take up your challenge.

You take three empty glasses and ten coins and spread them out on the table. "Here's the problem. That bloke Sid who always wins the quiz down the road said he'd give this tenner to anyone who could solve it." Place the tenner on the table too. The likelihood of anyone entrusting you with a tenner under any circumstances is negligible but this fact seems to bypass Einstein and Keith who are still drunk with victory.

"How can you divide the coins up so that they're all used and there's an odd number in each glass? I've got to tell you, it sounded simple when I first heard it but it took me ten minutes to work it out. Sid's bet that you can't solve it any quicker, and here's his tenner to prove it. Want to match his bet?"

You mentioned Sid because Keith and Einstein don't have a high opinion of him. They also don't have one of you so the thought that you solved the problem at all, never mind in ten minutes, will have them in fighting mode.

But when their ten minutes is up, they're going to have to hand over a tenner if they want to find out the answer, just like you had to hand over your pop and crisps at school for a lend of their homework. It's been a long while coming but it's payback time.

THE CATCH

The problem can't be solved in any mathematical way. Einstein and Keith are not going to be able to divide ten coins into three glasses and leave an odd number in each. But if you look at the problem from a different angle, with a bit of lateral thinking, you can come up with a solution. Put two coins in one glass, three in another glass and five in the third. That distributes all the coins but doesn't leave an odd number in each glass.

However, you rectify that by stacking the glass which contains five coins inside the one that has two.

If you count up, you'll see that each glass now has an odd number of coins in it. No one said anything about keeping the glasses separate. And funnily enough no one bothered to ask.

THE HOOK

"I don't know what it is, maybe when I banged my head as a kid, but I sometimes get these psychic flashes. Premonitions I think you call them." Marilyn knows all about premonitions. She's been having psychic flushes all her life, especially after a sweet sherry or two. So she listens with genuine interest, bless her. Keith, however, is sceptical.

Concerned by his cynicism, you offer a demonstration of your paranormal skills. "I bet I can send a thought into Marilyn's mind. No, not that sort of thought. It will be a word. I'll write a word down, concentrate on it and I bet Marilyn can guess what it is."

Keith is not sure what kind of stunt you're pulling but he's pretty sure that you haven't managed to set anything up with Marilyn ahead of time. You write something down on the back of an envelope, look at Marilyn as if concentrating and say, "Marilyn, in a moment I am going to ask you to think of a simple word. Don't worry, it's easy to spell. But I really need you to really concentrate if this is going to work."

Then you turn to Keith and say, "I'm pretty sure this will work. How about a little side bet? If Marilyn gets it right, you buy the drinks. If she gets it wrong, the drinks are on me?"

Keith won't have the faith in Marilyn that you have, which is a pity because Marilyn is about to have another one of her flushes.

THE CATCH

How can Marilyn possibly guess the word you have written down? By your cunning is the answer.

The word you write down is "NO". Write it in capital letters and make some extra fake movements with your pen so that it is not obvious to anyone that the word only has two letters. Now, to get Marilyn to call out this word you employ a very special method of questioning her.

You say "Now before we do this I have to reassure you that we've not arranged anything beforehand. I've written a word down on this paper. At the moment Marilyn, do you have any idea which word I've written down? Yes or No?"

And she will, in all honestly, answer "No." At which point you immediately turn over the envelope and show that she is correct.

Marilyn might not get the joke but Keith will. He'll also be getting the drinks in.

 GOT YOUR NUMBER

THE HOOK

Having proved Marilyn's talent for mind reading you kindly give Keith a chance to win his money back. "Just a bit of fun Keith but here's where you get your revenge. Remember though that this one's for real. And for a tenner of course."

You write something on the back on an envelope and place it writing side down on the table. "No words this time. I've written a number. A number between one and a hundred. Now, when I snap my fingers I want you to think of a number. Has to be between one and a hundred though. Understand?"

You're making a big performance of this. Taking control so that Keith only talks when you want him to. There's no time for joking around if you want to win this bet.

"And I bet I've written down the number you're going to think of. Only one condition. You can't change your mind. It's just like that quiz show on the telly; I can only accept your first answer. Got it?"

Keith's got it alright. "Okay, let's go." You snap your fingers, Keith thinks of a number and you win your bet. How?

THE CATCH

By more verbal dexterity that's how. When you snap your fingers you look at Keith and say, "Are you thinking of one?" And if he has been following your cues all along he will automatically respond by saying "Yes." You jump on that word, saying, "He thought of the number one," and then turn over the envelope on the table to reveal that you wrote down the number one.

Keith will immediately protest but as far as you are concerned his complaints go unheard. You repeat the conditions of the bet, that the first answer he gave is the only one you can accept.

16 STANDING ON CEREMONY

THE HOOK

In trying times people bond together. Friendship in the face of adversity. The spirit of the Blitz. Now you might think that having conned Keith out of his cash in the previous two stunts that he would be your worst enemy. But experience shows that the reverse is true. He's already lost his money. The best thing that can possibly happen to him is to watch someone else lose theirs. So when Einstein comes wandering up to see what's going on, you'll find Keith just standing by while you take his mate on a visit to the cleaners.

"Listen Einstein. I was just showing Keith here my remarkable psychic abilities. My mother says it's a gift. It would have to be, I never pay for anything."

A little humour, however naff, can work wonders in these situations. If Keith smiles, he's effectively giving you the go ahead to try a scam on his mate.

"It's uncanny really. Like that Spiderman; a sort of tingling sensation. Look, I'll show you. Think of a word and write it down on this piece of paper. Don't let me see it."

Einstein scribbles away. It'll probably be something with thirty-plus letters that no-one but him and the man that compiles the Oxford Dictionary knows how to spell. But don't let that worry you.

"Good, now put the paper on the floor, writing side down, and stand on top of it. We don't want anyone touching it. Laboratory conditions, this is."

"Now, I've just done this for Keith and Marilyn." You lie but it looks similar to what you've been doing so you won't get any argument from them. "And I'm getting everything spot on. No mistakes. What would you say if I could tell you what's on that paper? Before you speak, let me answer that for you. You'd say it's a miracle. But a miracle is what I'm going to do. My intuition is really rocking today so I'm prepared to bet a tenner that I can tell you what it is. Is it a deal?"

If he wavers, appeal to Keith and Marilyn. They might be friends with Einstein but they'd still like to see him taken down.

THE CATCH

What's on that paper? Well, Einstein is, of course. He's standing there like a right plonker with his feet on it and that's what you tell him. Time now to rely on your two strongest assets – an unnaturally thick skin and a selective deafness when it comes to people asking for refunds.

TOURIST TRAP

THE HOOK

English is a funny language. Has a lot of strange rules that make it difficult for even the natives to spell it properly. All that I before E except after C nonsense. Add to that the current fad for text messaging in which nothing is spelt properly and you have a language under siege. This bothers the likes of Einstein and Keith, who consider themselves sole defenders of the

Queen's English. Odd really because they break the I before E rule every time they write their names.

But it's during these alcohol-fuelled debates that you can introduce this little challenge. Point out how the American tourists seem to have problems with all our British place names. They are always talking about going to Ly-cester Square. Or Glow-cester. Or Edin-borrow. Most of them never quite get it right. In fact, there's one word that every American pronounces wrong – no exceptions. Every single one of them and you bet that neither Einstein or Keith can guess what it is. And you can find it in every English dictionary, a copy of which, by sheer coincidence, you happen to have with you. You throw the pocket dictionary onto the table along with your challenge.

Usual fees apply. Education doesn't come cheap.

THE CATCH

When they've given up calling out difficult words from the dictionary in bad American accents you riffle through the pages to the W section and put your finger on the word "Wrong."

"That" you say with confidence, and a very slight drawl, "is the one English word that every American pronounces wrong."

78 SPIN ON IT

THE HOOK

"Have you noticed how different coins have different sounds?" you say. You take out some change and start spinning it on the table as if proving something. So what? What you're actually doing is manoeuvring Einstein into a betting position. He's been there all evening talking with Marilyn and for the last half hour you and Mickey have been sitting with empty glasses and almost empty pockets. The last of your change is spinning like copper ballerinas on the table and adding it up you see that there's not even enough to buy a half between you. So you make your challenge.

"I bet I can guess the date on any coin Marilyn pulls out of her purse – without even seeing it. All she has to do it spin it on the table while I'm not looking and I'll get pretty close. Even if I'm not bang on, I'll guarantee that I'll be able to get closer than you Einstein." That's some bet and it's not long before you, Einstein and Mickey are facing away from Marilyn while she spins a coin on the table. Each of you has one guess at the date. Nearest to it is the winner.

THE CATCH

As you might have guessed, since you and Mickey are both brassic, you've contrived this little game together. Basically it's an ambush. Let Einstein call the date first and then you and Mickey call the year either side of it. The odds are that you or he will be nearest to whatever date is on the coin. You've agreed to share the winnings.

There's a tiny possibility that you might lose, but only if Einstein's guess is spot on. If that's the case, you only lose a fiver, since what you forgot to mention to your mate Mickey was that he shares the risk too. Got to be worth taking a chance at those odds though.

79 TRUST ME, I'M A DOCTOR

THE HOOK

This scam was used years ago by an eminent London gynaecologist. The gynaecologist used it to enhance his reputation and therefore his earnings. He appeared to have the uncanny knack of being able to predict whether his pregnant patients were going to have a boy or a girl. He was never wrong. Always right. And it was this remarkable feat that brought him a lot of wealthy clients.

You can use it to get yourself a reputation as a real Nostradamus as well as free drinks all year round.

THE CATCH

When this scheme was devised there was no known way of accurately predicting the sex of an unborn child. But the doctor in question would hum and haw and mumble some pseudo-scientific nonsense and then verbally predict the sex of the child and write it down in his surgery diary.

When the child was born the client would come back to visit the doctor. Half the time they would congratulate him on his powers of prognostication, bring gifts and spread the word of his seemingly uncanny knack. The other half of the time they would say: "Well you said that I was going to have a boy but I actually ended up having a girl. I guess you can't be right all the time and at least it was healthy."

At this the doctor would look amazed, saying: "No, no. I definitely said you'd have a girl, not a boy." And then he'd open up his diary, turn to the date of their consultation and point out his prediction. This was because he always wrote down exactly the opposite of what he told them at the time, so the prediction was always correct – if he was right with his original verbal guess than he didn't bother showing them the diary on their post-natal visit!

And that's what you do. Whatever you tell someone, write down the opposite in your pocket diary at the time. You can actually use this devious system to place wagers on all kinds of events. Elections and championship boxing matches are particularly good bets; the only criteria is that there are only two possible outcomes and that it is sufficiently far ahead in time for your punter to have conceivably forgotten which option you originally guessed. Sorry, predicted.

80 HELD FOR QUESTIONING

THE HOOK

"Hey guys, that Marilyn is as clever as she is cute." This will be news to Keith and Einstein but you continue. "She could whip both of you in a quiz. In fact I'd bet money on it."

This is highly unlikely since Marilyn thinks that quiz is spelt with a 'k', followed closely by a 'w'. But, her spelling skills aside, you continue to defend her intellect, much to their annoyance.

Five minutes later and the dynamic duo are locked in a battle of brainpower with Marilyn. To everyone's surprise, they lose! You, as usual, win.

THE CATCH

What we're talking about here is a rigged quiz. Questions are written on small slips of paper and then drawn out of an ice bucket. Since you pull the questions out, Marilyn gets the easy ones while Keith and Einstein end up with problems that Stephen Hawking would struggle with.

The trick is to know which question is which and you do this by folding them differently. The slips of paper that have difficult questions are folded in half, the easy ones into quarters.

You write all the questions in secret. Or better still prepare them at home. Then tip them into the bucket and pull them out one by one. The way the papers are folded make it simple for you to pick out difficult questions for the brainy bunch and easy questions for Marilyn.

Now it won't be long before Keith and Einstein start to whinge. But that's why you have been extra cunning in compiling the questions. You see the ones you wrote for Marilyn are easy for her to answer but not for anyone else: Her mother's maiden name, where she went to school, her first pet, etc. If they complain, just read one of them out, adding Marilyn's name and saying, "Okay then, where did Marilyn go to school?" They'll eventually shut up. And pay up.

FIVE
PARTY ANIMAL

"THERE ARE TWO WAYS TO
MAKE MONEY FROM YOUNG PEOPLE:
ENTERTAIN THEM OR CHEAT THEM."
- MARGARET WISEMANN

81 SITTING TARGET

It's party time. All your mates are here but it looks like a Night of the Living Dead reunion. A few party tricks; that's what this place needs. Something to catch the attention of the tasty redhead sat with the musclebound gym-monkey.

You could try this one on Dave but he looks as though he's already comatose so it wouldn't be much of a challenge. Anyone who's sitting down will do, but if you don't want to expend too much effort then pick someone smaller than yourself. That mate of Dave's, Baz. He'll do.

First thing is to get Baz to put his drink down. Then ask him to sit up, back straight, just like he was taught at school. Here's the challenge. You bet that he can't stand up from his chair in one movement without using his hands.

Let him try. It's easy enough. Bend legs, push up, keep the back straight, hands out of the way, don't move your feet. It's not particularly easy, but it's not impossible. "Okay, try it again, but this time I bet I can keep you in that chair using just one finger." You extend the forefinger of your right hand and flex it in a puny attempt at a display of strength. "One finger and you won't be able to get up. Ready?"

You flex your finger once more and press it lightly against Baz's forehead. You count to three and ask him to get up. Amazingly, he can't.

THE CATCH

As long as Baz adopts the posture you describe, he'll find it impossible to stand up if you press down on his forehead.

One point to watch is that the chair he's sitting on doesn't permit him to move his feet under his body. An armchair is ideal. People don't normally pay attention to the way they stand up. What they are doing is shifting the centre of gravity by moving the body forward and the feet backwards. Normally the hands help push the body up from the chair too. Take all those aids away and you can render them incapable with the lightest touch.

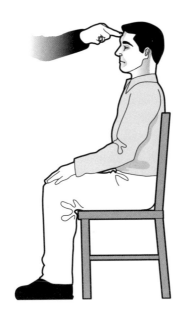

82 PUSHING YOUR LUCK

THE HOOK

Wait a minute. The talk is getting all metaphysical now. Must be the drink. Or the boredom. But Marilyn's been wittering on about spirits and other worlds and Jim, who seems to be recovering from his tequila frenzy, is telling everyone how it's all true. Yes, multiple dimensions, how do we know what's real and what's not? All cobblers but it makes a good introduction to this next bet.

"You're right. It's all a matter of perspective. A Tibetan monk showed me this once. It was amazing." You pull out a business card from your pocket. Not yours, of course. Doesn't do to leave any evidence. You fold it, tear a small hole in the middle of it and then open it out again.

You peer through the hole at Marilyn as you say, "Yep, a Tibetan mystic showed me this. He could push a real person right through a hole this size. Unbelievable huh?"

"Bloody nonsense," someone will say, quite rightly, and that's the person you make the bet with. "No, really, it can be done. I've seen it. I bet I can even do it myself. Ten pounds says I can push Marilyn right through this little hole, right here, right now, without tearing the card."

And with the money handed to Mickey for safekeeping, you proceed to do just that, push Marilyn through that tiny hole in the business card.

THE CATCH

Tibetan monk my arse. All the mumbo jumbo is just dressing to lead them off the track and antagonise some poor sap into calling you a liar. More fool them as you make good on the bet by placing the business card against Marilyn's forehead and then prodding her through the hole with your index finger. You are *pushing her* through the hole and if you push hard enough she'll soon tell you to stop. No illusion there.

Smile as you do this one. You've just taken the rise out of someone you hardly know. If you laugh it off, they should too. Doesn't matter how hard they laugh though; they're still not getting their money back.

83 THE MONEY PIT

THE HOOK

That stunt with the hole and the business card is a winner. It's corny as hell but everyone's had a drink so they don't mind. As usual you pretend to feel a little bit guilty so you offer the punter a chance to win his money back.

"I'll tell you what," you say, throwing three coins onto the floor. "Look at the hole and look at the coins. All you've got to tell me is which coins will fit through the hole and which ones won't. And I won't make the hole any bigger than it is now."

Sounds easy enough. There's a penny, a twenty pence and a two-pence piece. That two-pence piece will never fit through. It's obvious. It's also very strange because you've just bet him that if he can tell you which coins will fit through the hole, you'll give him back his tenner. But first, he has to put another tenner to match the bet. I hope he's brought plenty of cash with him.

THE CATCH

The punter will lose the bet because, strangely, all the coins will fit through the hole. It is an amazing thing to watch because you're about to put a large coin through a small hole.

With the penny and the twenty-pence piece you have no problem. The hole, if you've made it right, is slightly larger than the twenty. They drop straight through. To get the two-pence piece through you adopt a different handling.

First you fold the card in half.

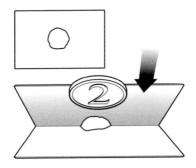

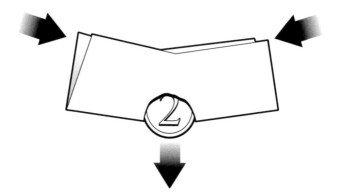

Then you drop the two pence piece inside so that part of it rests inside the folded hole but will not pass through. Next you push the corners of the folded card inwards. This results in the hole expanding in one direction. It has the same circumference but it is being squashed so that the diameter stretches. It will become large enough to allow the two pence piece to drop right through. The only thing to make sure is that the card you use is thin and flexible. Instead of a business card you can use a train or lottery ticket or anything similar.

The guy who paid out the tenner should consider it money well spent because he'll sure as hell be trying it at the office tomorrow.

84 CUT AND RUN

THE HOOK

Now's the time to lighten his wallet even further.

"I was just kidding. The fact is that I really can make a hole in a card and crawl right through it. Some say it's a mind over matter thing. But I say it's just dedication, healthy diet and a pure heart."

That should bring the sneer of derision that it deserves. But you persist with your claim. First though you need a postcard and some scissors. Dispense a minion to find them while you keep your bankroller in plain sight and talk up the bet some more.

"Yep, I bet that I can cut a hole in this card and crawl right through it. None of that fake pushing stuff. I'll start on one side of the card and I'll crawl right through it to the other."

You're offering a real freak show tonight and no mistake. And with the postcard and scissors in hand, the punter's going to need to put up the price of a ticket.

THE CATCH

In this bet you fulfil your promise to the letter. You really can cut a hole in a postcard (or any similar size piece of paper) big enough to climb right through.

To do it, though, you need to cut the hole in a very special way. Firstly you make a horizontal slit as shown

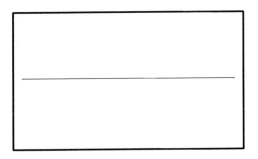

Fold the card in half along the line of the slit and then start to cut straight lines across it from the top almost to the bottom. Between

these you alternate with lines cut from the bottom almost to the top. Make the cuts as close together as possible. It's a fiddly job but there's a tenner at stake so take your time.

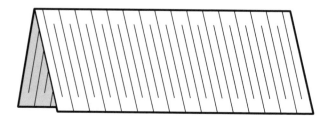

Now gently open out the card and you'll find that you now have a large loop. Handle it gently as it's very fragile and will break easily. But, if you're careful, you will be able to drop it over your head and slide it right down around your body.

85 PICKUP PUTDOWN

THE HOOK

That gorgeous redhead still hasn't noticed you. And the gorilla she's talking to has already arm-wrestled everyone in the room and performed press-ups resting on one little finger for the amusement of the ladies. He's sitting at the table letting her feel his pecs. He's a babe magnet and it's beginning to annoy you because the nearest thing you've got to a six pack is the pile of empty cans next to you.

Never mind, there's one way you can share the limelight and make a few bob on the side. You guessed it, it's time to move on to pastures new and pull a few more scams.

Tap The Hulk on the shoulder and ask how much he weighs. Don't be surprised if he knows exactly; that sort of person usually does. Tell him you thought he was heavier than that – that'll worry him. They always want to be heavier. Then look at the chair, look at him, and say

"I bet I can lift you with one hand."

"What?"

"Lift you. And the chair. I bet I can reach down, grab that chair leg with one hand and lift you right off the floor. For at least thirty seconds."

He will stare at you like the nutter you're doing a good impression of. Especially if he remembers that you couldn't open the peanuts earlier on. But you look him straight in the eye and repeat your challenge. "Yes, I reckon I can do it. Lift you and the chair, straight up." Then wink at the redhead, and look back at him. Open your wallet, take out a ten spot and whack it on the table as you say "If I'm wrong, you owe me a tenner. Is that fair?"

It's the equivalent of a slap round the face with a wet fish and his tenner will soon be on the table right next to yours. In a moment, they'll both be cuddling up together in your wallet.

THE CATCH

Okay, get ready for this. If you want that tenner you need to put on a performance that De Niro would be proud of, should he ever be seen dead at a party in Croydon. With the money down, stand next to The Hulk's chair and eye it up as if judging just how you are going to make the lift. Caution him:

"Hey, hands off the table, no cheating. This is hard enough as it is. If I'm wrong, you owe me a tenner, and that's a tenner I'm not going to lose."

Look slightly mentally unstable at this point. Take off your jacket. Flex any muscles you can find. Snap a crisp in two or burst a balloon as a warm-up. Grunt a bit and a crowd will start to gather. Explain the challenge to them. Don't begin the lift until you have plenty of people watching – they might come in useful later.

With your audience around you, repeat the challenge a final time to the Hulk: "Remember; if I'm wrong, you owe me a tenner." Now for the big sell. Kneel down by his chair. Put out your hand, grab the chair leg and lift. Not too hard or you'll get a hernia. Just pretend to lift, because let's face it you haven't got a cat in hell's chance. But it's all in the acting, as you step back and say "Okay, last chance. You owe me a tenner if I'm wrong." Appeal to the crowd like Kylie flashing her backside. They'll cheer you on, especially the redhead, women tend to go for feeble-minded men facing impossible odds.

Now by this time anyone normal might have twigged what's going on. Even the redhead might be giving a little giggle. But a man that spends too much time in a mirror-lined gym isn't listening. Pretend to lift again. Not too hard. Then step back, wipe your brow in mock exhaustion and say

"Okay, I admit it, I *am* wrong… you owe me a tenner! " Pick up the money, put on your jacket and slowly walk away. It may take a moment before he realises what happened. But the crowd will suss it immediately. Which is good because they are the only thing that stops him from lifting you off the floor with one hand.

86 AGAINST THE WALL

THE HOOK

At last you've got some attention. Unfortunately it's mostly from the would-be Schwarzenneger whose money you've just filched. You suggest a rematch to even the score, reminding him of the old phrase "See a penny, pick it up, and all the day you'll have good luck." In this case the penny will be replaced by his tenner, which will prove to be anything but lucky for him.

"You look like you do a lot of exercise. This should be a cinch for you. You can have your money back from the last bet if you can pick it up off the floor." Sounds too easy. Naturally there are a couple of conditions, the first being that he matches the money you are kindly putting up for this wager. The other rules concern the specific way he's got to do it.

"First, you stand upright." This could be a bit of stretch for the Missing Link. "And to make sure you are, stand over there, heels and shoulders touching the wall." Lead him over and make sure he assumes the position, pressing him back if you need to. Place the tenner on the floor right in front of him.

"Second, you don't move your feet and you don't bend your knees. It's a straight pickup from the floor. Got that?" If he's done any gym work at all, he'll not think that's much of a challenge. The guy knows he can touch his toes without wincing. Picking up money off the floor shouldn't be a problem. Should it?

THE CATCH

This works well on any gym-monkey because it's much harder than it sounds. You place the note just a few inches in front of them. Recap the points about standing straight against the wall, keeping their feet in position, and especially not bending at the knees. Then, on the count of three, ask them to try to pick up the tenner. If your instructions are followed properly, they will not be able to do it. Gravity will topple them over before they get any where near the money.

It looks so strange that within minutes the rest of the room will be trying it. And you'll be sorry you didn't make the bet with all of them.

 87 HAND OVER FIST

THE HOOK

If you're feeling brave, you might want to play The Hulk at one more game before sending him on his way a broken man. Ask him to clench his hands into fists, assuming he's not already doing that, and place one fist on top of the other. The thumbs are on top.

"Now hold them there. I'm going to try to separate those fists no matter how hard you try to keep them together. I get three tries. Then you get three tries with me. The wager is that I'll be able to manage it and you won't."

Since The Hulk is twice your size it would appear to be another bet in his favour. Surprisingly, you separate his fists first go. Oddly enough, he doesn't seem to be able to separate yours at all.

THE CATCH

Before you try this bet you should make sure that you haven't intimidated him enough so that he uses this bet as an excuse for a full-on punch-up. It's not worth it for a tenner.

But if he's up for some fun, you'll find that no matter how big he is, it's very easy to knock his fists apart. You just hit the back of the upper one firmly with your strongest hand. Slap it sideways and it will come off the top of the other fist. Don't punch though; otherwise he's liable to punch you back twice as hard.

The reason he can't knock your fists apart is that you cheat. As you put your right fist on top of your left, you secretly extend your left thumb and grasp it in your right hand. The thumb locks the fists together and a single blow won't be able to separate them.

 FEET UP

THE HOOK

If the partygoers are laughing, you can get away with almost anything. Alcohol and laughter are an effective lubricant for the wallet. No one minds paying for a good time and so when you offer to use your hypnotic powers to glue someone's foot to the floor, you'll find no lack of takers.

"It's true. It's a sort of magnetic influence. I just make a few mystical passes over your leg and your foot will stick to the floor."

When someone daft or drunk enough to accept the bet has put themselves and their best foot forward, stand them with their side against the wall. "It's safer this way. Because sometimes the magnetic forces weaken the other foot and you might fall down." This is bull but you need to set up the conditions under which the bet will work. "If you feel yourself falling, you can hold onto the wall." Sure.

Gemma rushes forward to offer her appendages for the demo and you start making mysterious passes along her leg, commanding it to become "heavy, very heavy" as if trying to hypnotise her shapely limb. And no matter whether she's wide awake or blind drunk, when you finally snap your fingers and give the command, she won't be able to lift her foot from the floor. And all done without the aid of a nailgun!

THE CATCH

This is another stunt that uses the punter's centre of gravity against them.

The mystical mumbling is all nonsense but it's still important. To work the bet successfully you should use as much showmanship as you can manage. If people believe you are using hypnosis, the trick works even better.

Obviously hypnosis isn't actually necessary at all. It's the positioning of the punter that's vital. She should be standing with her right side against the wall. The side of her right foot is against the skirting board. Her right shoulder touches the wall. This is supposedly to make sure she's upright and, as mentioned earlier, to stop her falling over. The real reason is to make her stand with all her weight on her right foot.

It's the left leg that you pretend to hypnotise, waving your hands up and down it like a demented Tommy Cooper. Build dramatically to the actual moment, saying "When I count to three, I'll snap my fingers and I want you to try to lift your left leg. But no matter how hard you try

you won't be able to lift it without falling over. Here we go: one, two, three!"

Snap your fingers and shout "Now! Your foot is stuck to the floor, your foot is stuck to the floor, your foot is stuck to the floor." The repetition helps unnerve her and when she tries to lift her left foot, she won't be able to without falling over. Like the gent that you are, you'll be there to grab her. And her boyfriend's cash.

 STOLEN KISS

THE HOOK

Her bloke will be regretting backing his fiancée to take part in one of your daft stunts. Time to put that animosity to good use. Get someone to find a sheet of newspaper. Lay it on the floor and make your next bet as the leggy Gemma picks herself up off the floor and re-adjusts her skirt.

"I bet that I can stand Gemma and any man here on this sheet of paper and yet he won't be able to kiss her. Gemma on this side of the paper, him on the other. Both facing each other. And yet, after a few magnetic moves, he won't be able to plant a smacker on her lips."

Now Gemma never was one to put up much of a struggle so even at a tenner you won't be short of volunteers queuing up to have a crack. But both her lip-gloss and your cash are safe.

THE CATCH

Once again, no magnetic powers are in effect. It's 100% scam. As soon as you have a challenger you lead him, Gemma and the newspaper over to the nearest doorway. Place the paper on the floor in the middle and ask Gemma to stand on the far end of it. Close the door on her. The challenger stands on the newspaper too, but on the near end, this side of the door. With the door between them, you've just created one of the world's most effective contraceptives. You've also just won the bet. They're standing on the same piece of paper, face to face, and yet no kiss will come to pass. Her boyfriend should be grateful. Maybe even enough to forget the tenner you took off him.

90 TRIAL SEPARATION

THE HOOK

Gemma's being a good sport as usual and so you decide that there's room for another challenge with another kiss and another tenner at stake.

"No doors this time. Just my mystic powers of hypnosis. Gemma, I want you to raise your hands like this and place your fingertips together. Good. Here's the challenge. I'm going to make a few more mesmeric passes and I bet that no man here will be able to pull Gemma's hands apart. Any takers?"

The Hulk would be a good bet for this but he's probably smarting too much already from his ritual humiliation. If people are slow in coming forward, up the stakes by saying "and there's a snog in it for any man that succeeds. From Gemma, obviously!"

Again it seems like an easy bet to win. Gemma is perfectly proportioned but definitely on the petite side. So when some lumbering lothario offers to take up the challenge, it looks like Gemma will end up swapping spit after all.

THE CATCH

When the punter steps forward, position Gemma so that her hands are fingertip to fingertip. Her arms are bent and raised so that her elbows are almost shoulder height with her hands at the same level inbetween. Ask her to press her fingertips together as hard as she can, as you make some more of your phoney mystic passes as if to imbue her with supernatural strength. If the guy is ugly enough, that should provide her with some motivation. If not, give her a wink and promise her half your winnings.

The guy is to grip Gemma's arms at the wrists. Tell him to take hold and try to pull her hands apart. He's not allowed to suddenly jerk them apart. He must use strength, not surprise, to separate her hands. That's the only condition.

No matter how hard he tries, even the biggest guy won't be able to budge her, and no-one will be more surprised than her. Unusually for Gemma, the more the guy tries to separate her limbs, the more determined she will be to keep them together.

91 GETTING THE NEEDLE

THE HOOK

Should anyone take your claims seriously, and never underestimate people's capacity to believe in utter bull, they might ask you about the way hypnosis is used to do all sorts of other marvellous things. Controlling pain for instance. It would be unethical for you to demonstrate pain control on a human subject, even if they have been anaesthetised by nine pints of lager. If, however, someone would care to find you a needle, you might be persuaded to give an alternative demonstration of your otherworldly powers.

You also need a few balloons; at a party they should be readily available. Grab a few and when the needle arrives make another bet.

"I can hypnotise this balloon so that it will feel no pain." If you've got a marker pen to hand you might want to draw a face on the balloon. It's a bit of showmanship that will draw a bit more sympathy and appreciation from the hard of thinking. "This is Bob the Balloon," you say, bobbing the balloon up and down for emphasis. "And this is a needle, sworn enemy of balloons the world over."

Hand the needle to someone stood nearby and the balloon to someone else; preferably someone of a nervous disposition whose sudden death might create an amusing diversion. Ask the person with the needle to stick it in the balloon. This will take some coaxing, especially of the person who's holding the balloon. When needle and balloon meet there will be the prescription bang. Bob is no more.

"A terrible tragedy, I think you'll agree. But I bet that, using hypnosis, I can stick the needle into a balloon and it won't go bang. Wanna see me do it? For a tenner?"

THE CATCH

Everyone is so used to the fact that if you stick a needle in a balloon it will burst that they don't think it could be any other way. That is, everyone apart from the 'smart alec' who remembers the old trick from their schooldays in which you secretly stick a piece of Sellotape to the balloon beforehand and push the needle through that. But that would be cheating, you point out, and you would never stoop to such underhand methods – you're about to do it without any external aids or safety net.

The secret is where you stick the needle. At the top of most balloons,

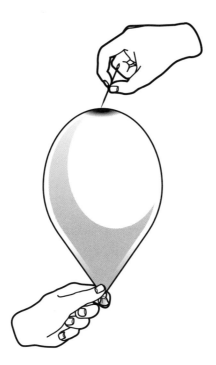

opposite the neck, you'll find that the rubber is considerably thicker and less taut. That's where you stick the needle. You've got to insert the needle carefully and slowly but you'll be amazed the first time you try it.

The needle goes through the rubber and the balloon doesn't pop. It doesn't pop when you take the needle out either; it just deflates slowly as air pours out of the hole you just made.

Look around for the right type of balloon before you make the bet. You want one that's not inflated to its full capacity. And be sure to find someone really wimpy to hold the balloon the first time round. It all adds to the fun and once again the people who are laughing aren't thinking too much about how much money they're losing.

THE HOOK

While the crowd are on a scavenging expedition you may as well get them to pick up a few pencils along the way too. Ask someone to hold one of them at each end and then ask someone else to lend you a ten pound note. You should have wads of the folding stuff by now but you just tell them that they would think that you were cheating if you used your own money.

While you were learning your psychic skills and the secrets of hypnosis from Tibetan monks you were also fine tuning your martial arts skills. You became so adept at them that you can shatter wood with nothing more than a creased banknote.

You fold the ten pound note in half lengthways and hand it around for scrutiny. "It's just a tenner. But the edge is keen. So keen that when I strike it against that pencil, it will slice through it like a knife through butter."

It's a dramatic claim and anyone looking at the note and pencil will doubt it immediately. Doubt it enough, you hope, to make a wager.

THE CATCH

This is a joy. One of the best feats of skill around. There's no way that you can strike the pencil with the tenner and break it in two. But there is a way that you can fake the entire thing and here it is:

You hold the creased tenner between your finger and thumb. Make sure your punter is holding both ends of the pencil as firmly as possible. After a couple of practice swings you slowly raise the note in the air and then equally slowly bring it down towards the centre of the pencil. Make it look as if you are gauging the exact spot at which to make your strike. Then raise the note high again.

This time give out your best Bruce Lee yell and bring the note down quickly against the middle of the pencil. What they don't see is that, as the note descends, you quickly stick out your forefinger so that it's hidden behind the note. It's the forefinger which actually breaks the pencil in two. The faster and harder you do it, the easier it is.

You won't believe how amazing this looks until you try it. As soon as your finger goes through the pencil, curl it back against your thumb and hand the note out for further inspection. I've seen people totally shocked when they see this performed for the first time. It really is that impressive.

93 HANDS DOWN

THE HOOK

Sit someone down and place their right hand palm-up on the table. Their forearm is horizontal and their upper arm vertical.

The challenge is for them to lift their hand from the table and then place it back palm downwards without rotating their wrist. It might not be entirely clear what you mean so let them try it first, and every time they rotate their hand at the wrist, point out that it's not allowed. "No, the challenge is to turn your hand palm down without rotating your wrist.

You could for instance, stand on your head and put your hand on the table that way. But that's another thing you can't do. You've got to stay sat down and manoeuvre your hand so that it ends up palm-down instead of palm-up."

This will drive them nuts. If they've never seen it before it seems utterly impossible. But it can be done.

THE CATCH

It helps to pretend that you're a robot for this one. Imagine that your right arm is mechanically hinged with no rotating joints. That's the way to defeat this strange challenge. It takes six moves to get your hand from palm up to palm down. Follow carefully:

 Raise your hand towards you so that it's at shoulder height, fingers almost touching your shoulder.

 Chop the hand down to the left, flat against your body in a vertical plane, with your elbow as the hinge. The finishing point of the move is with your forearm extended horizontally across your waist with your fingertips pointing left.

 Swing the forearm outwards horizontally until it extends straight out at ninety degrees to the waist.

Once again bring the hand up towards the shoulder as in Step 1. The difference this time is that the palm of the hand is now facing left.

 Bring the hand down across the front of your body once again, as in Move 2. This time the hand finishes palm down at waist level with the fingers pointing left.

 Keeping the upper arm still, swing the forearm out so that it points straight out horizontally from the body. This is just like Move 3 except you'll find that the hand is now palm down. Place it on the table. The challenge is complete. The hand has been moved from palm up to palm down without rotating the wrist.

THUMBS UP

THE HOOK

A game of Simple Simon. You'll give anyone ten pounds if they can do exactly as you do. But if they can't, they can expect a forfeit. Guess what that will be? There doesn't appear to be any particular difficulty to this challenge. You hold both arms out straight at shoulder height; they do the same. You turn your hands over so that the backs are facing each other. They do the same. So far so good.

Then you put one hand over the other and interlock the fingers, as in the prelude to the old "Here's a church, here's a steeple" routine.

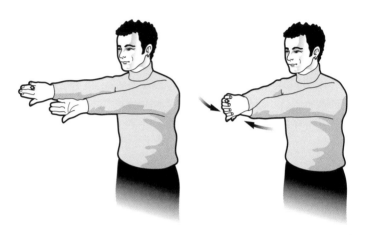
Awkward but not difficult. What happens next though will leave the punters gasping. Very slowly you rotate your hands at the wrist, turning them so that the thumbs are now pointing upwards.

Absolutely no-one in the room will be able to follow this manoeuvre. Even putting their hand in their pocket to pay you will be far less difficult.

THE CATCH

If you followed the instructions you gave the punters, you wouldn't be able to do this challenge either. Unusually for you, you cheated.

Give your instructions in the traditional Simple Simon manner: "Simon says – hold your hands out. Simon says – clasp your hands together," etc. While the punters are interlocking their fingers, you casually separate your hands again, using your right hand to gesture to someone at random, saying "not so high; a bit lower." Keep your left hand extended though. The seemingly helpful comment is just a bit of misdirection, because when you place your hands back together you don't place them back in the same position.

Instead, as it moves back, the right hand rotates a hundred and eighty degrees clockwise so that although the palm is facing to the right and the thumb pointing at the floor as before, the elbow is now pointing downwards. Before you separated your hands, it was pointing upwards. The right hand reaches under the extended left hand and the two hands clasp together once more, the fingers interlocking. This looks like the same position that all the punters are in. But it's not.

When you have both hands clasped you tell everyone to get ready for the final move – it's worth a tenner. "Simple Simon says – bring your thumbs to the top." You do exactly as you say, rotating the hands slowly in an anti-clockwise direction bringing the thumbs to the top. Give them a waggle when they get there. And expect a big laugh from the punters, because they'll suddenly realise that they just can't follow you. Now who's simple?

95 TONGUE TIED

THE HOOK

This is a great party game. Everyone throws some money into the pot and in return they're given a long piece of cotton. They put one end of the cotton in their mouths and let the other end dangle down to the floor. Hands have to be kept firmly clasped behind the back.

The object of the game is to eat the cotton as fast as possible. They don't have to swallow it. In fact they'd be stupid to. No, all they have to do is chomp the thread up into their mouths. Whoever gets the thread into their mouth first wins the game. It's a test to see who's got the best tongue coordination. Who at a party could fail to be captivated by that?

And when the game gets underway you see those people who really are orally adept. Look at how quickly they can wind that thread up. Gemma in particular is putting in a fine performance, yet you remain calmly detached. In fact you've not even started on your thread yet, but you'll still win this game in the most unexpected manner imaginable.

THE CATCH

Anyone trying to wind the cotton up with his or her tongue is doing it the hard way. You can bide your time while all the tongue twisters reel their lines in. People will wonder why you are simply standing there with a piece of thread hanging from your mouth and not making any attempt to play. Instead you cheer your punters on, giving them every encouragement.

But, when it looks like someone is about to win, you play your masterstroke. You purse your lips around the thread and suck in a deep breath. This will hoover up the thread so fast that it immediately disappears from view and ends up inside your mouth. It's a stunning thing to watch. And it takes but a second to make you the winner.

They'll be choked; just make sure you're not.

96 DRESSING DOWN

THE HOOK

They're a well-dressed lot at this party. Nice to see that they seem to have made a bit of an effort, but it's all a little bit too reserved for your liking. Time to loosen things up a bit, and where better to start than with Jim, a man whose idea of a wild night is undoing his top button.

"That's a nice jacket Jim. Very nice. Looks a bit tight on you though. And heavy. In fact I bet you can't take it off, alone and unaided, in less that thirty seconds."

Now Jim knows that he can get his jacket off in less than thirty seconds. It's his trousers he has trouble with. Especially after three halves of cider. And although he had a close encounter with one of those big funny cigarettes the students gave him earlier, he's feeling much better now and feels that he can easily beat your challenge. Thirty seconds? He'll manage it in ten. Just got to shake it off the shoulders and let it fall clean off his arms. He's thinking that it's you that must have had a few sherbets too many. Ah, but perhaps there's a catch; maybe you're planning on grabbing hold of him to stop him getting the jacket off?

"Don't worry, no-ones allowed to touch you or your jacket; they're not allowed to obstruct you – or help you either for that matter." Fair enough. Game on.

THE CATCH

As soon as someone says "Go!" Jim will take off his jacket but he'll wonder what the hell is going on when you take yours off at the same time. The answer is in the wording of the bet you made. "I bet you that you can't take your jacket off, alone and unaided."

He's not doing it alone because you've taken your jacket off too. There really is one born every minute.

97 GET KNOTTED

THE HOOK

Now that Jim's taken his jacket off you can relieve him of his tie too. Hand it to someone and ask them to tie a knot in it. "Very good. But did you notice that you had to use both hands to do it and that you had to put one end of the tie through a loop to make the knot?"

Of course they did – the mob are thinking "so what?" so you attempt to stimulate their interest by pointing out the obvious even further. "It's completely impossible to tie a knot without letting go of the ends. Try it." And for the next five minutes let everyone have a go at making a knot in Jim's tie without letting go of either end. It just can't be done. Such a thing would defy the laws of physics. At least that's the conclusion they reach after trashing Jim's tie. The laws of physics, however, are just one of the many laws that you break with disdain on a regular basis. The rules are laid down, the cash hits the table, and in less time than it takes to say "what a swizz", Jim's tie does indeed have a knot in the middle and everyone, while not exactly blown away by your technique, has to admit that at no time did you let go of the ends.

THE CATCH

It's perfectly true that if you take hold of a tie, or a piece of rope or string, by each end, it's impossible to make a knot without letting go of one of them. Except for one tiny loophole, and that's if you make the knot in your arms before you pick up the tie, then transfer it!

How? Easy. Lay the tie on the table in a straight line. Now fold your arms and bring your hands down to the table one at a time, taking hold of an end in each. Now, as you slowly unfold your arms, a knot will appear in the middle of the tie. It might not be the most impressive display, but we'll take their money first; their adulation can come later.

98 TIE MASSAGE

THE HOOK

After your punters have seen you work *Get Knotted* they might think they're a little wiser, albeit poorer, for the experience. They're astonished at your nerve, however, when you offer to repeat the stunt, but with the following conditions: "This time I won't fold my arms. I'll hold the ends of the tie before I start. I'll make a proper knot. No play on words. And you can check everything to make sure it's absolutely fair and square."

You can let the punters interrogate you for ages on this one and you're able to meet pretty much all their conditions. But the knot will stay in their imagination until they plonk down their money. After that, it will become frustratingly real.

THE CATCH

This is clever. You really will tie most of the knot while not letting go of the ends of the tie. It's only at the end that you employ a little swindle to make the impossible possible. Let's start with the moves.

Take the tie and hold it between your hands. Keep your left hand still and move your right hand over the left and back under so that a loop of the tie is draped over your left arm as shown.

You'll see that two gaps are formed at A and B. Your right hand now takes its end through gap A, around the middle of the tie and comes back out through gap B, without letting go.

Slowly move your hands apart and you're left with the tie looped around each wrist, criss-crossing between your hands. So far the punters have seen you do some nifty if strange-looking manoeuvres. At least it looks as if you're trying to tie an impossible knot. But it isn't quite there yet. You need the punter's assistance to make the bet work.

"And just to be sure I don't do anything sneaky, I want you to grab hold

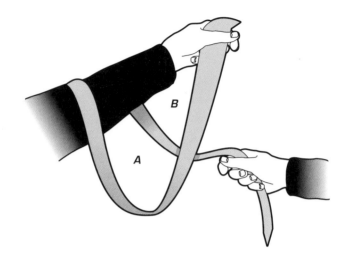

of each end of the tie." Let him take one end with his left hand and the other with his right. Supposedly you are handing the tie to him so that it's completely under his control. What he doesn't know is that, in doing this, he's just helped make the knot.

Leave him with the tie and them ask him to stretch it out between his hands. He'll be amazed and dismayed when he finds that there really is a knot in the middle.

99 PHONEY

THE HOOK

The party's almost over and it's time to settle a few scores before you leave. Main thing you need is that redhead's 'phone number but how do you go about getting it? She's the cutest girl in the place, but no-one has a clue who she is. Suddenly you have an idea. A little scam that'll serve two purposes.

You start by talking about the sensitivity of women and how they're generally more tuned into spiritual matters than men. And that if you take a little time, you can, because you've practised, psychically home in on a woman's thoughts. Just like that Mel Gibson movie. There'll be doubters in the room so you offer a demonstration.

"It needs to be someone I don't know. How about you?" you say, pointing to the redhead. I'm not going to ask you anything about yourself, but I'd like you to think of something that I couldn't possibly know. Your mobile number will do; write it down here. Don't let anyone see it." You give her a pen and something to write on.

Then you ask her to sit on a chair, the information face down on the table in front of her. "What you've got to do is relax. Just concentrate on the number and I'll call upon the spirits to whisper it to me. Maybe we could have the lights down for this?"

Turning the lights down doesn't raise any spirits but your own. Nothing like a romantic atmosphere though for what will soon become a very intimate drama between you and the object of your desires.

In five minutes time, the redhead will be convinced that the two of you have a psychic bond, you'll have her 'phone number, and the bloke next to her who bet you that you wouldn't get it will owe you a tenner. How's that for a ménage à trois?

THE CATCH

Remember the set up. The paper with the girl's telephone number on it is on the table, writing side down. She's sitting with her hands resting on the arms of the chair.

You start with some psychic nonsense in an effort to convince her that you do indeed possess strange powers. Stand or kneel directly in front of her. Extend the forefingers of each hand and gently tap her on her hands. "Can you feel that?" Course she can.

Move your hands along to her forearms and stroke her there. "And can you feel that?" She says yes again, quite rightly wondering what you're up to. Ask her to close her eyes, and then move to her upper arm and stroke her there. "And that?"

You continue the intimacy (or intimidation, depending on which way you look at it), both hands moving at the same time and tapping her gently on the shoulders with more questioning. Then you stroke the sides of her head. Finally you place each forefinger gently on her eyelids. At least that's what she thinks you've done as you've been touching her with both hands throughout. What you've actually done is asked her to close her eyes and extended the forefinger and the little finger of one hand and placed them on her eyelids, leaving your other hand free.

With the free hand you put your finger to your lips to silence the party crowd so that they don't give the game away. While the girl has her eyes closed you pick up the piece of paper from the table and read her phone number silently to yourself.

As soon as you've memorised it, turn it writing side down again and bring your left hand up in front of her face. Extend your left forefinger as you remove your right fingers from her eyelids and move both hands away from her face at the same time. Simultaneously fold in your little finger and ask her to open her eyes.

The first thing she sees is your hands moving slowly away from her face, both your forefingers extended. If you play it right, she'll still be assuming that you had one finger from each hand touching her eyelids. She has no idea that you could have seen the writing on the face-down paper. Ask her to hold your hand for a moment while you have another one of your funny turns, staring a lot and mumbling while you pretend to contact the other side to find out the number she's written down. Repeat the number you memorised aloud, all except for the last digit, saying "We don't want everyone to know, do we?" The rest is up to you.

100 GET SHIRTY

THE CATCH

It's the end of the night and you've taken them for everything apart from the shirts on their backs. Now there's an idea.

Surely not even you though could get the shirt off someone's back while they were still wearing their jacket, could you? You'd better believe it.

Einstein doesn't believe it for a second. "There's no way you can get someone's shirt off without them taking off their jacket first!" And Keith is soon joining in, demanding proof.

Baz agrees, so does Jim and a few of the others and pretty soon you have a revolution on your hands with everyone putting down money to see you take the shirt off a man's back, like that isn't what you've been doing all night. Keith, egged on by Einstein, demands you put your money where your mouth is. And no tricks this time.

"Okay, I'll take you all on. Level odds. And Einstein, it's your shirt I'm having so brace yourself." With some reluctance Einstein sits down and lets you undo the collar and cuffs of his shirt "Because when this comes off, you don't want your buttons flying everywhere."

"Step back lads. This is it." No one moves. Surely, you're not really going to pull his shirt off? Everyone's certain that you're going to pull some silly sleight of hand or talk your way out of it. What you're definitely not going to do is pull that shirt off...

My God! There's a collective gasp as you grasp the shirt by the collar and pull it clean away. Who's the daddy?!

THE CATCH

You've been building up to this all evening and you haven't disappointed. And it's all thanks to Einstein because you and he are in cahoots. Yes Einstein, your former enemy, has suddenly become your accomplice. Well, he wasn't

happy about catching Keith snogging with Marilyn; she's been his girl since school. With revenge on his mind it didn't take much to convince him to go to the loo and prepare for his starring role.

The preparation is easy. Your stooge takes his shirt off and puts it back on by draping it over his shoulders like a cape. He fastens the buttons down the front and the cuff buttons around his wrists but leaves his arms out of the sleeves. He then puts his jacket back on top as normal. If he keeps the jacket buttoned, no-one will be able to see that he isn't wearing the shirt properly.

The real art is in persuading someone to place a bet, and your stooge has a hand in that too, egging on the punters. When you apparently turn the tables on him and choose him for the stunt, no one will suspect that you've set up the whole scenario.

Don't be surprised if you see your stooge pulling a few stings of his own next time you're down the pub though; the buzz you get from pulling off a good scam can be addictive. But then you've probably realised that by now!